Building the Transcontinental Railroad

written by **Joeming Dunn**
illustrated by **Rod Espinosa**

magic wagon

visit us at
www.abdopublishing.com

Published by Magic Wagon, a division of the ABDO Publishing Group, 8000 West 78th Street, Edina, Minnesota 55439. Copyright © 2009 by Abdo Consulting Group, Inc. International copyrights reserved in all countries. All rights reserved. No part of this book may be reproduced in any form without written permission from the publisher.
Graphic Planet™ is a trademark and logo of Magic Wagon.

Printed in the United States.

Written by Joeming Dunn
Illustrated by Rod Espinosa
Edited by Stephanie Hedlund and Rochelle Baltzer
Interior layout and design by Antarctic Press
Cover art by Rod Espinosa
Cover design by Neil Klinepier

Library of Congress Cataloging-in-Publication Data

Dunn, Joeming W.
    Building the transcontinental railroad / written by Joeming Dunn ; illustrated by Rod Espinosa.
        p. cm. -- (Graphic history)
    Includes index.
    ISBN 978-1-60270-180-9
    1. Railroads--United States--History--19th century--Juvenile literature. I. Espinosa, Rod.
    II. Title.

TF23.D83 2008
385.0973'0903--dc22

                                        2007051655

TABLE of CONTENTS

Timeline

1825 - In England, George Stephenson engineered one of the world's first railway locomotives.

1830 - Peter Cooper finished America's first steam locomotive.

1841 - The first settlers moved westward.

1848 - Gold was discovered in California, setting off the gold rush.

1860 - Theodore Judah declared Donner Pass as ideal for constructing a line through the Sierra Nevada.

1862 - On July 1, Congress passed and Lincoln signed the Pacific Railroad Act.

1863 - The Central Pacific Railroad in California and the Union Pacific Railroad in Nebraska broke ground for a transcontinental railroad.

1864 - The Sand Creek Massacre occurred on November 29.

1865 - The Union Pacific Railroad reached the 100th Meridian, and was granted the right to continue on.

1867 - British chemist James Howden began manufacturing nitroglycerin on-site in the mountains for the Central Pacific. On June 25, Chinese workers went on strike.

1869 - On May 10, the Central Pacific and Union Pacific railroads joined together.

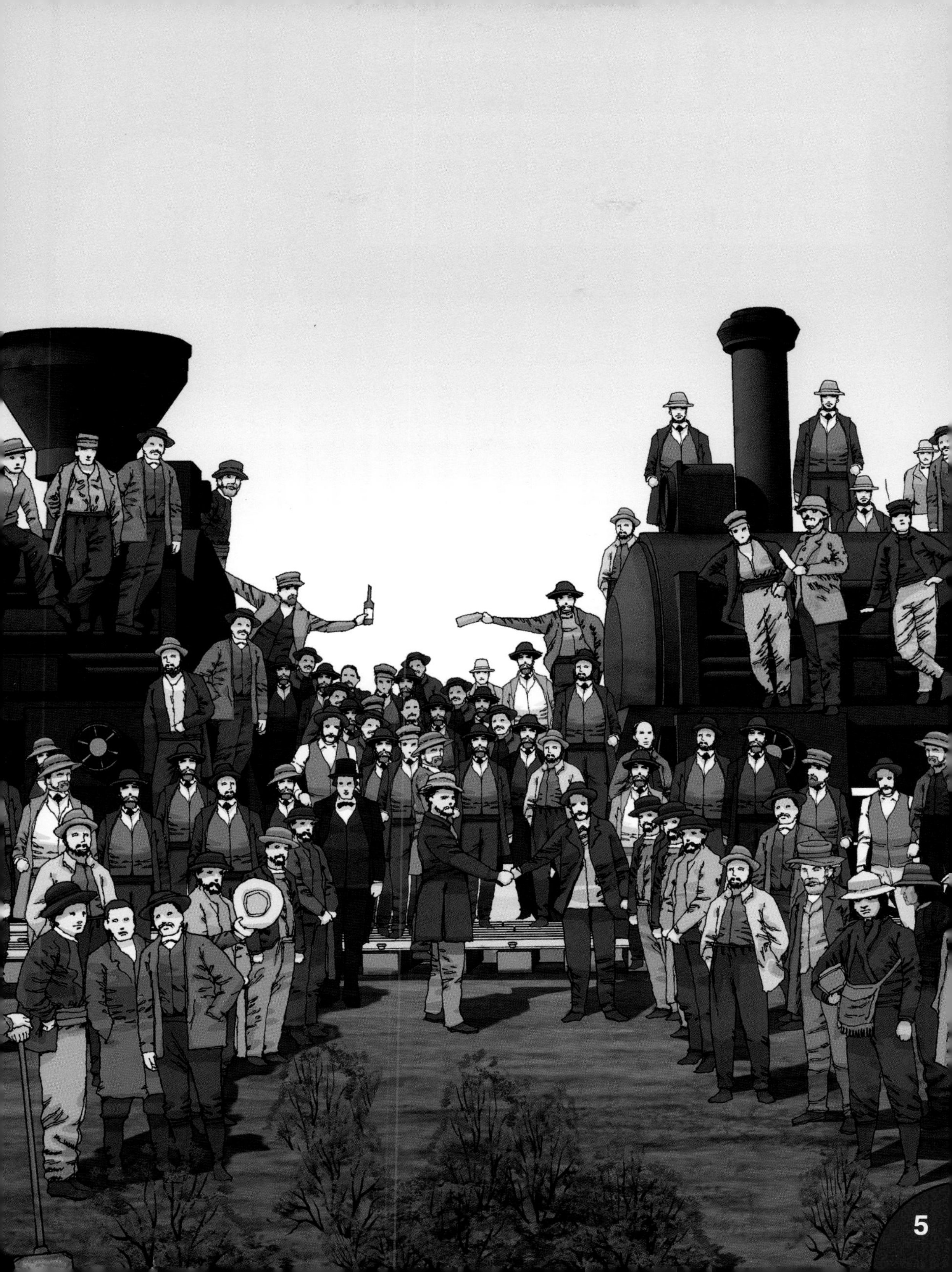

Chapter 1 Westward Expansion

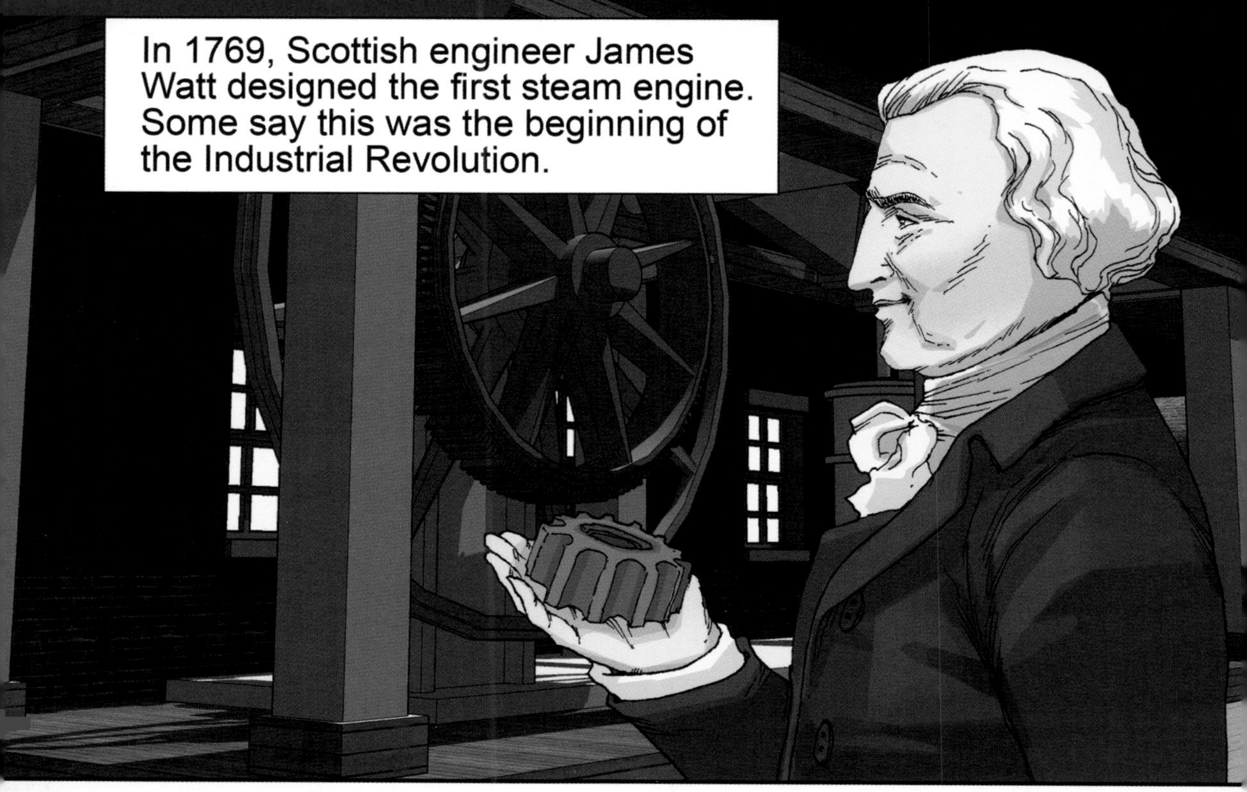
In 1769, Scottish engineer James Watt designed the first steam engine. Some say this was the beginning of the Industrial Revolution.

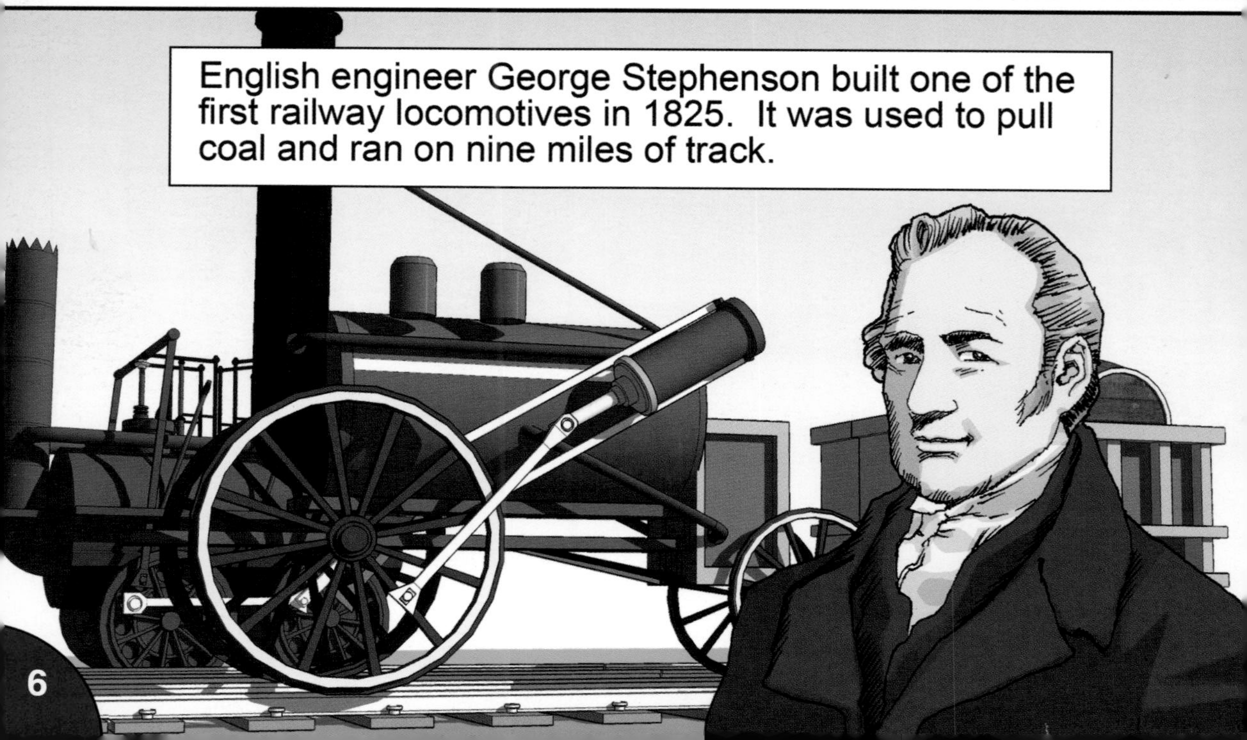
English engineer George Stephenson built one of the first railway locomotives in 1825. It was used to pull coal and ran on nine miles of track.

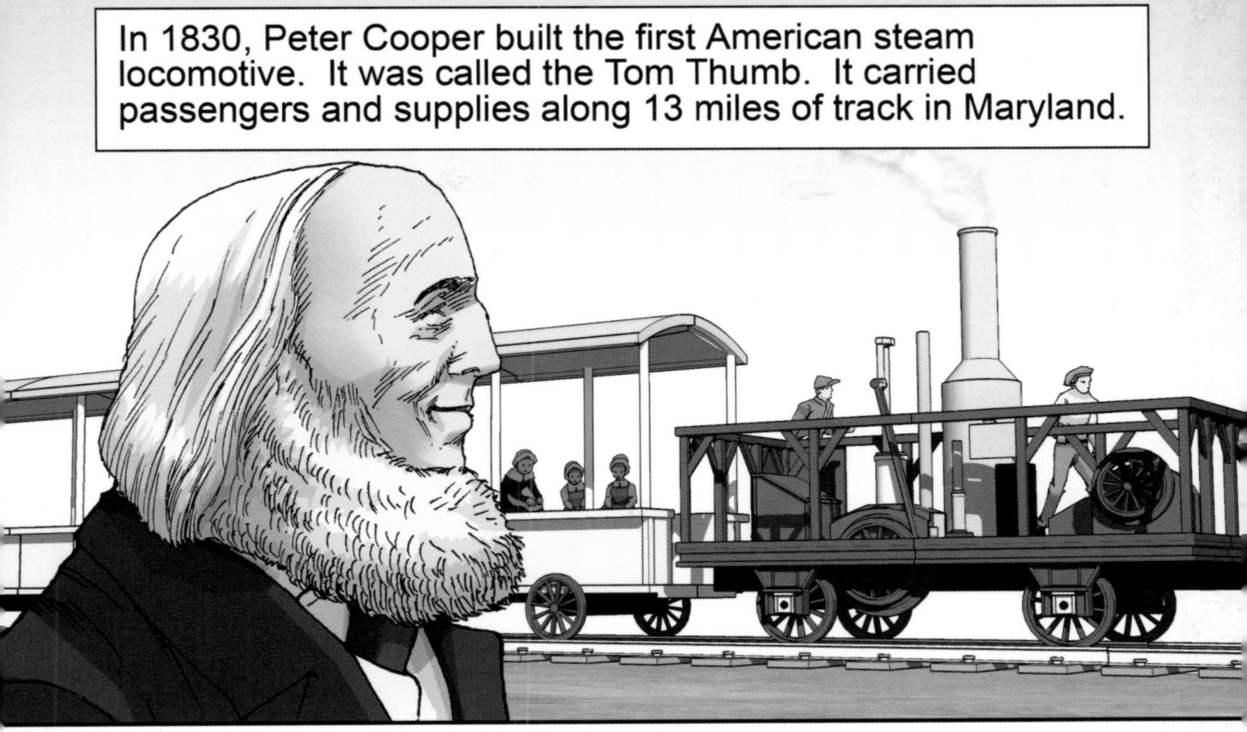
In 1830, Peter Cooper built the first American steam locomotive. It was called the Tom Thumb. It carried passengers and supplies along 13 miles of track in Maryland.

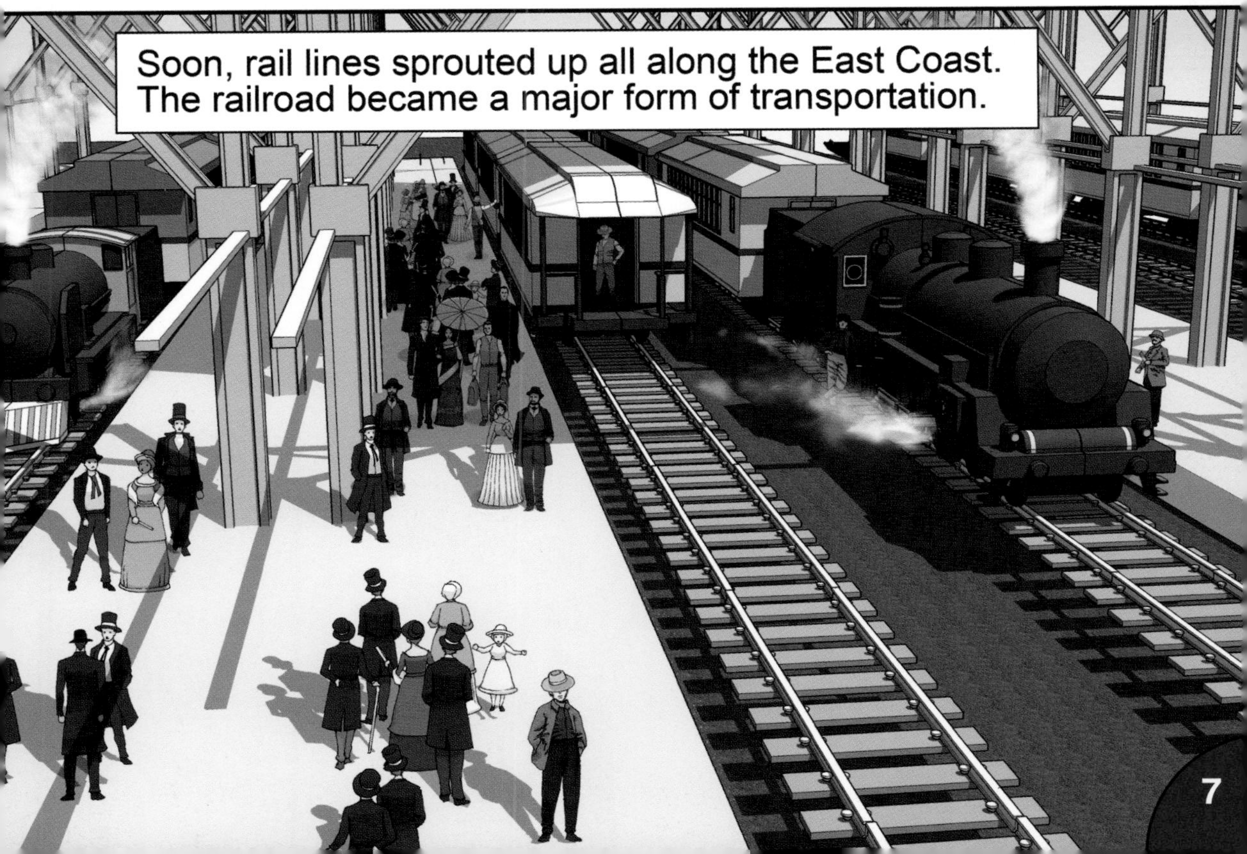
Soon, rail lines sprouted up all along the East Coast. The railroad became a major form of transportation.

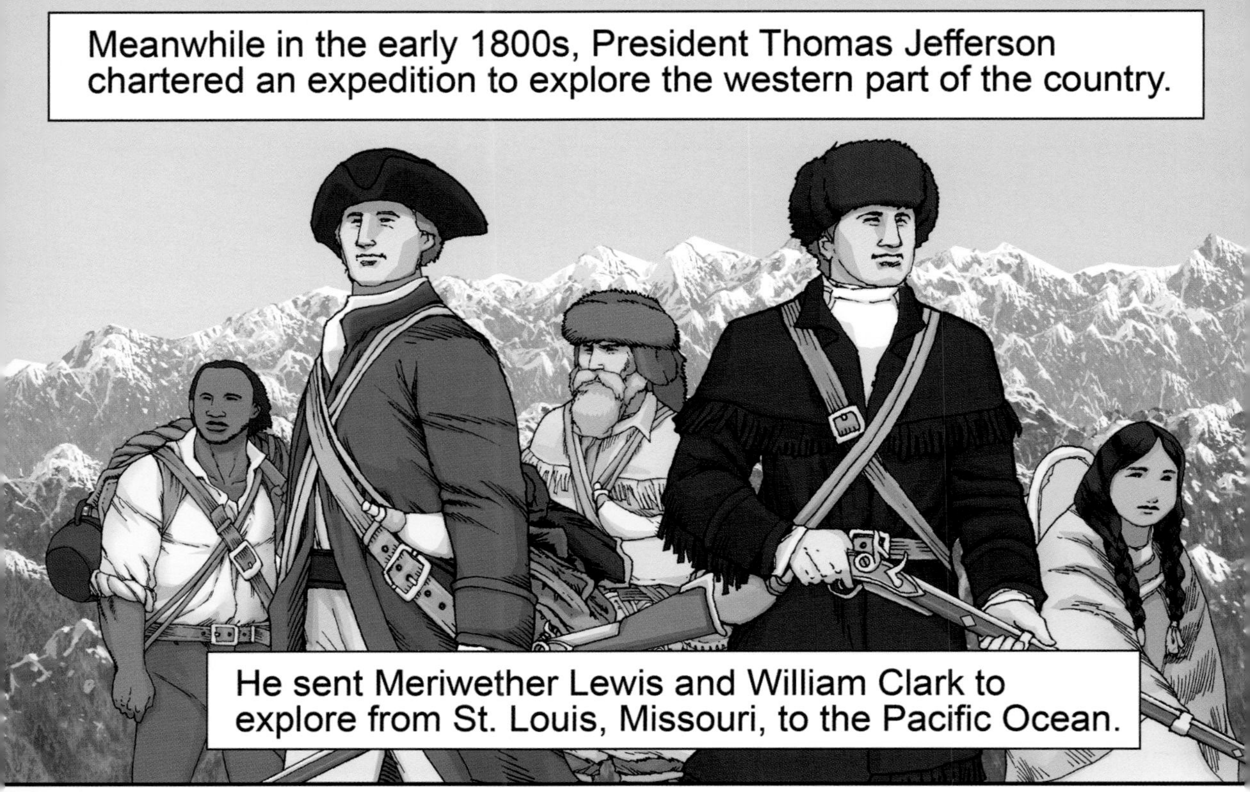
Meanwhile in the early 1800s, President Thomas Jefferson chartered an expedition to explore the western part of the country.
He sent Meriwether Lewis and William Clark to explore from St. Louis, Missouri, to the Pacific Ocean.

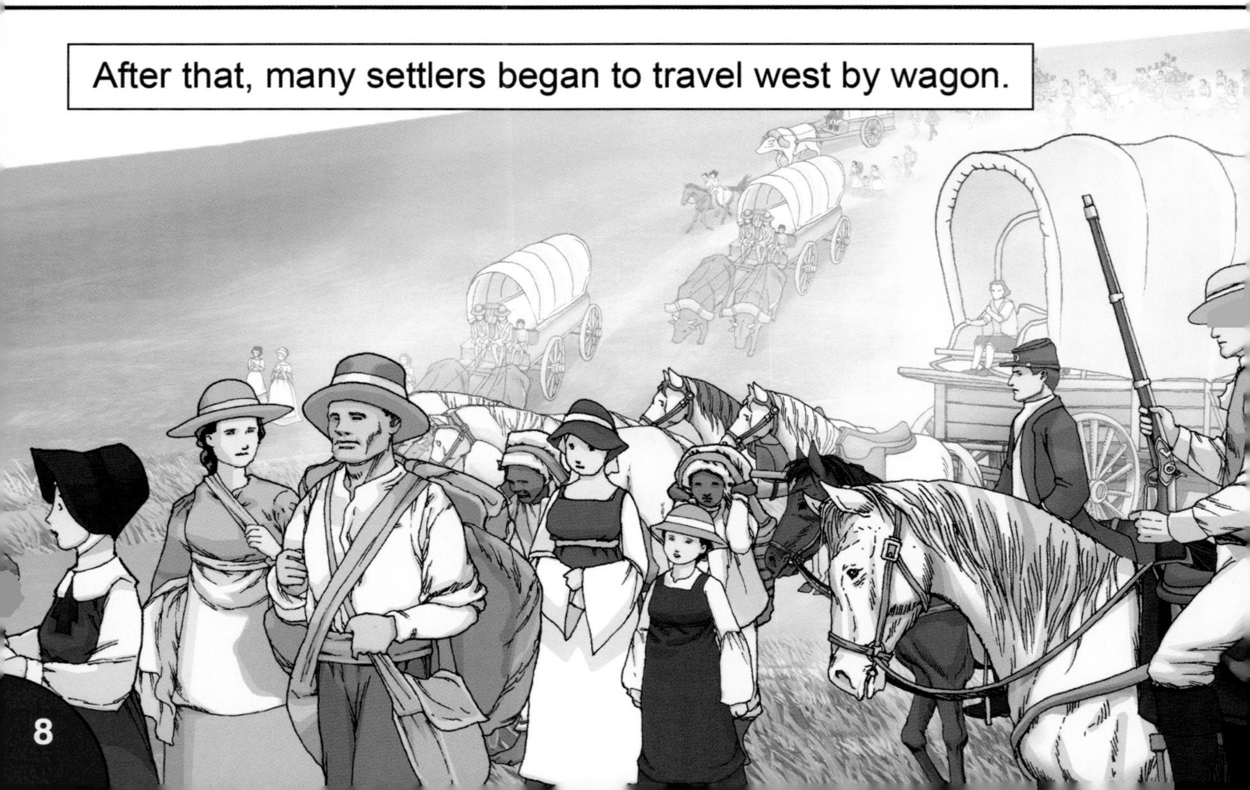
After that, many settlers began to travel west by wagon.

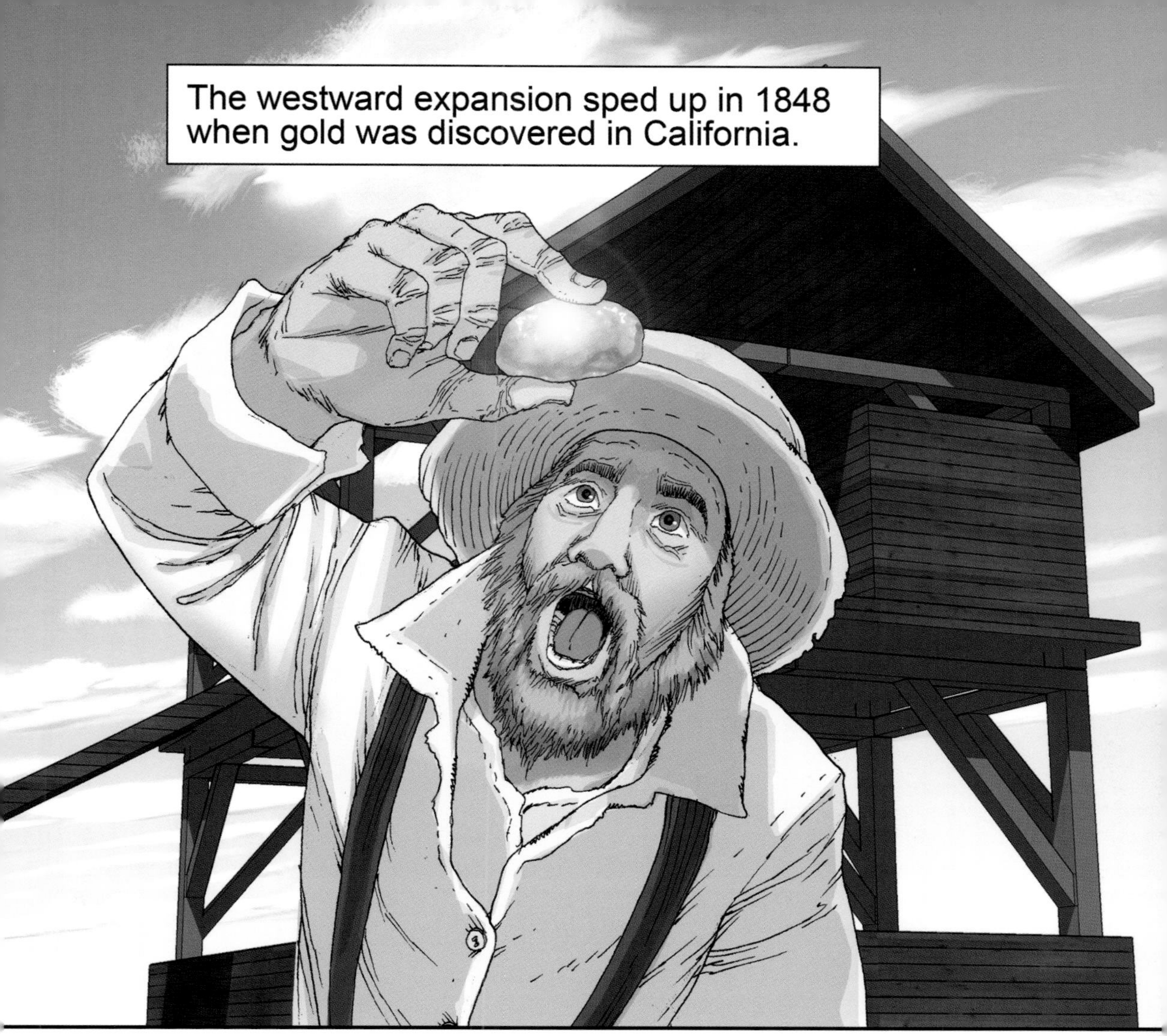
The westward expansion sped up in 1848 when gold was discovered in California.

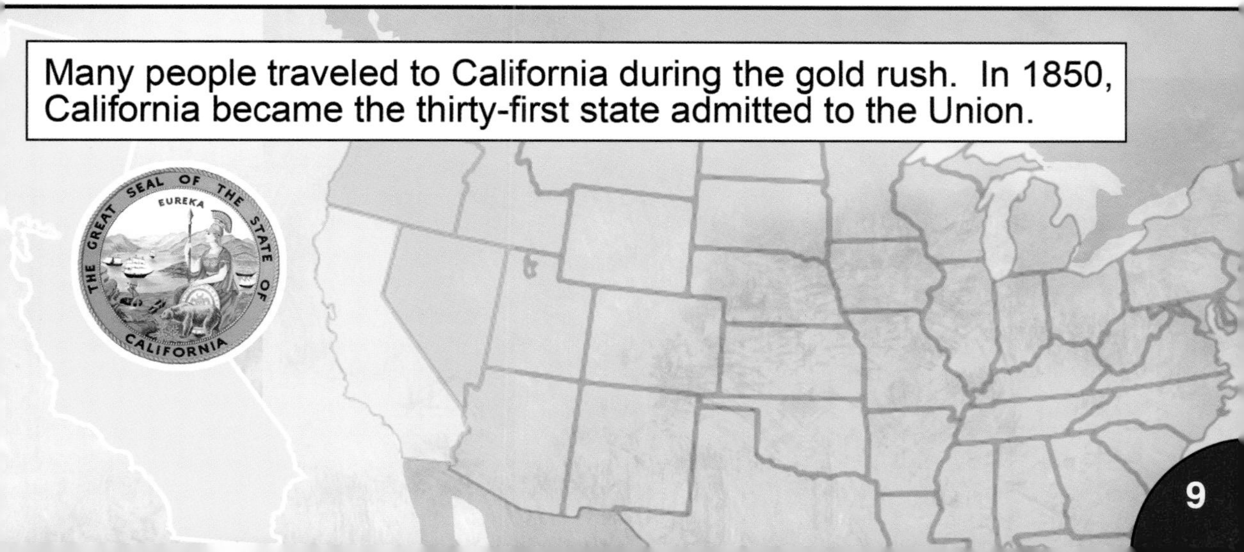
Many people traveled to California during the gold rush. In 1850, California became the thirty-first state admitted to the Union.
THE GREAT SEAL OF THE STATE OF
CALIFORNIA
EUREKA

Chapter 2 Central Pacific and Union Pacific Railroads

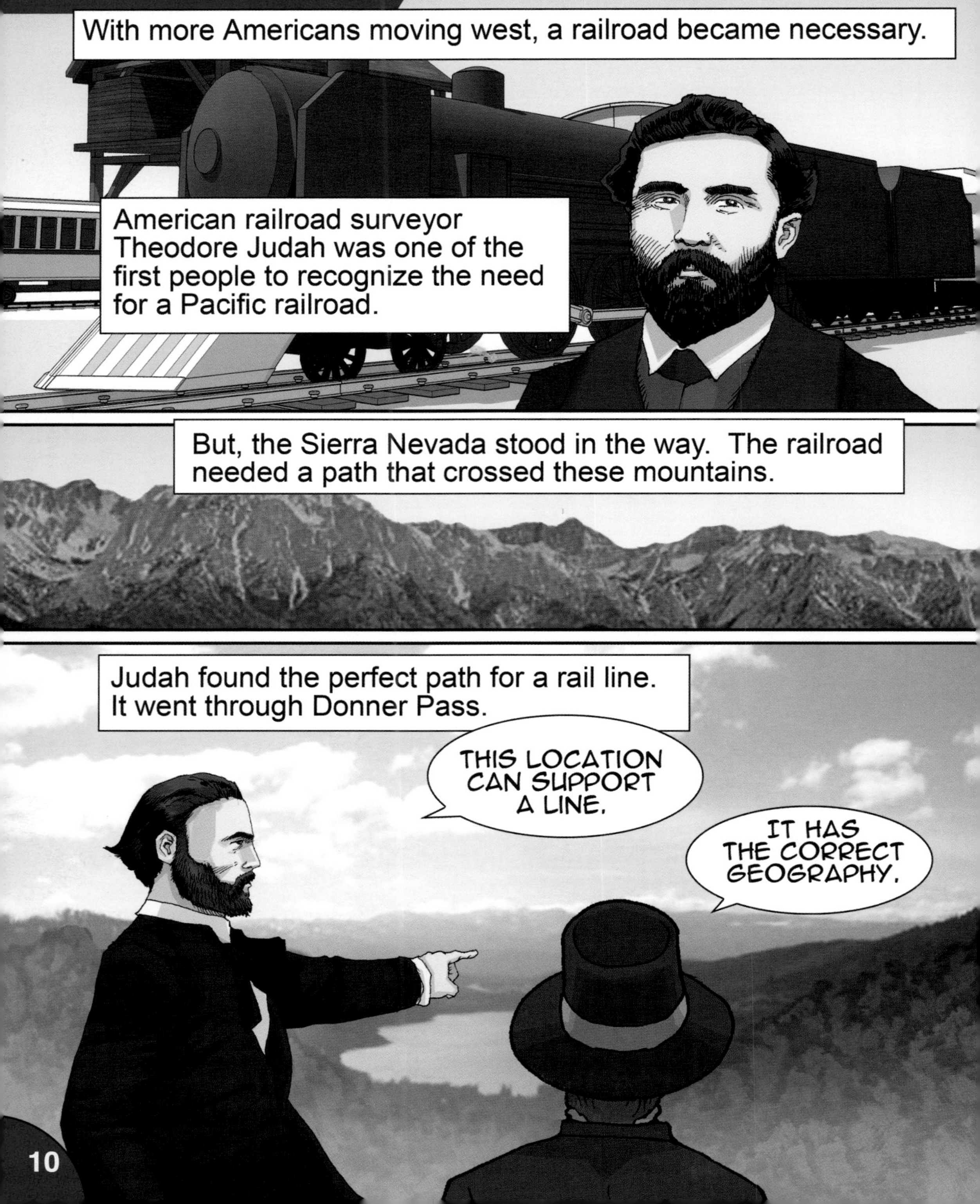
With more Americans moving west, a railroad became necessary.
American railroad surveyor Theodore Judah was one of the first people to recognize the need for a Pacific railroad.
But, the Sierra Nevada stood in the way. The railroad needed a path that crossed these mountains.
Judah found the perfect path for a rail line. It went through Donner Pass.
THIS LOCATION CAN SUPPORT A LINE.
IT HAS THE CORRECT GEOGRAPHY.

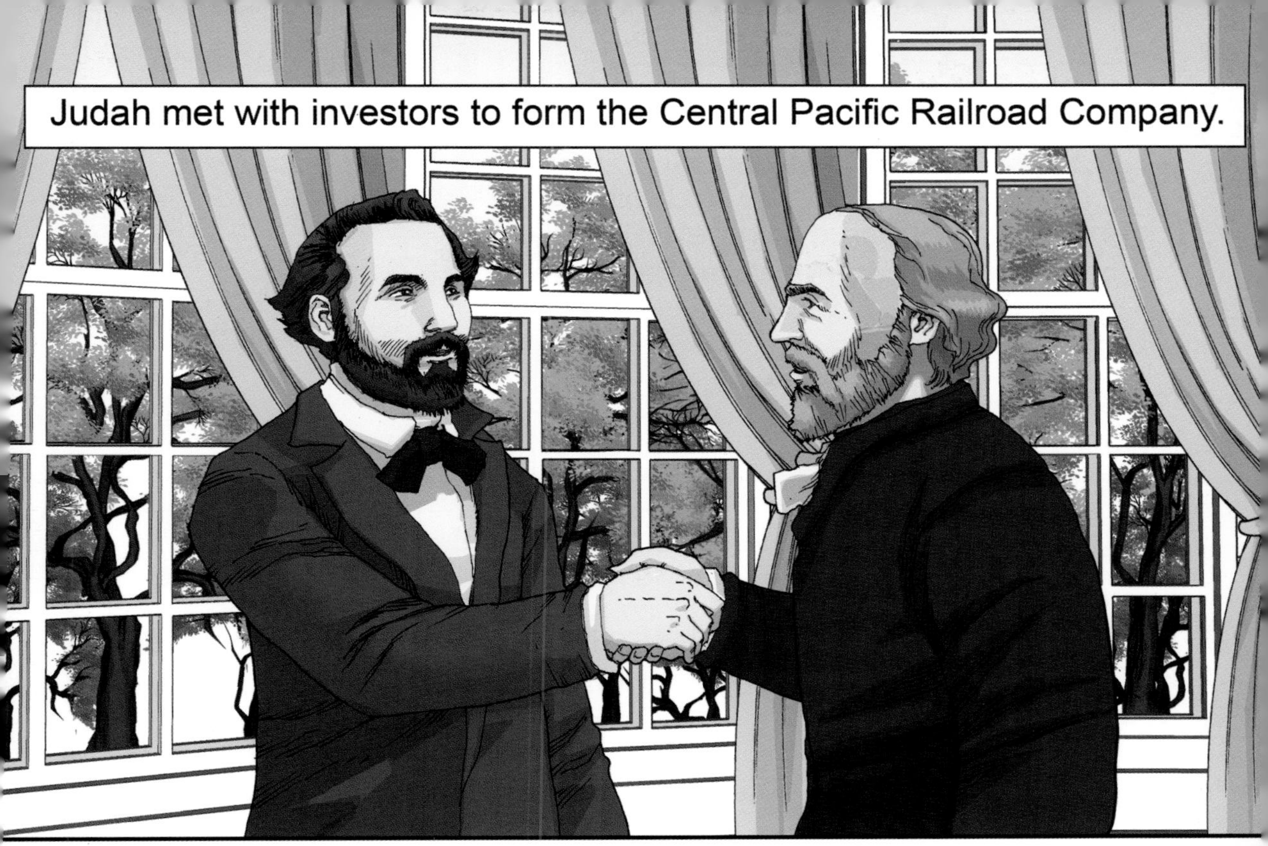
Judah met with investors to form the Central Pacific Railroad Company.

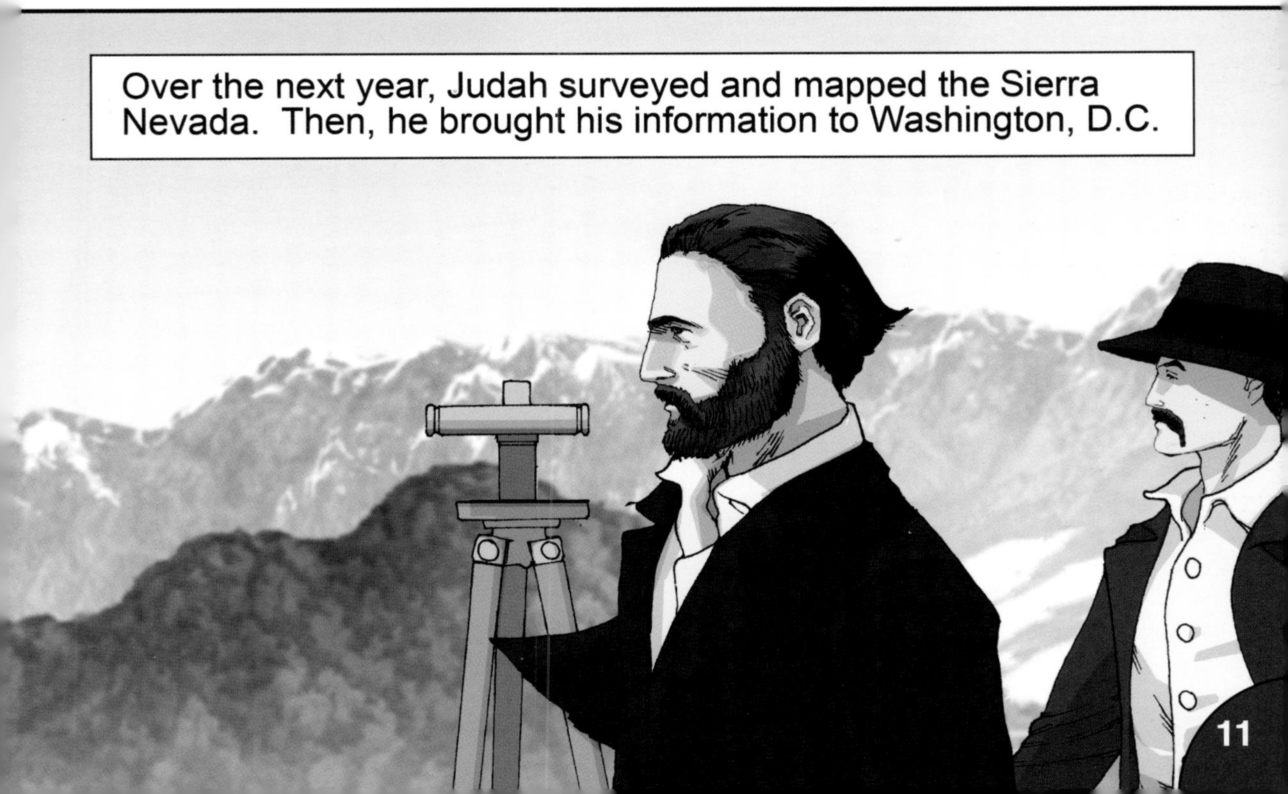
Over the next year, Judah surveyed and mapped the Sierra Nevada. Then, he brought his information to Washington, D.C.

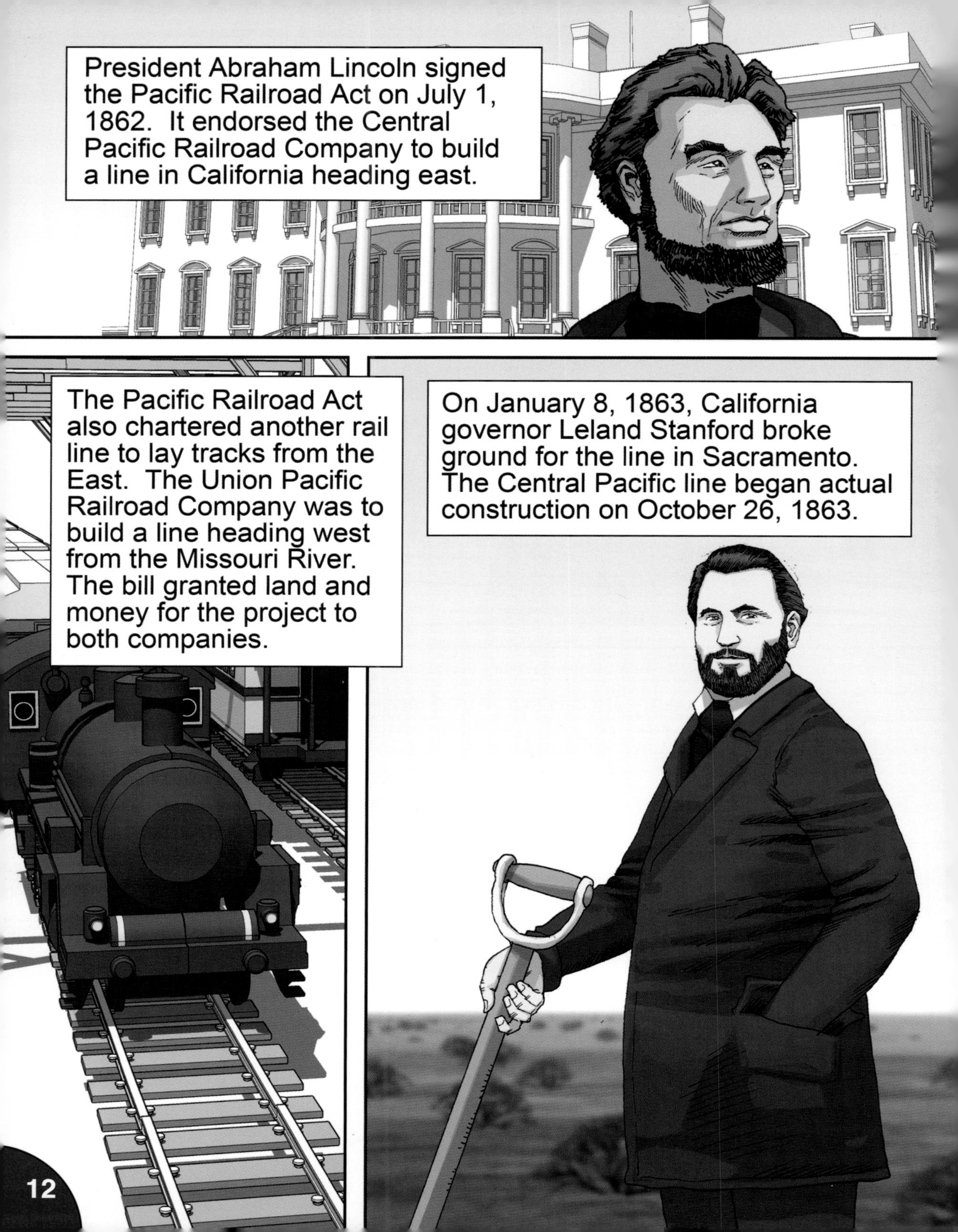
President Abraham Lincoln signed the Pacific Railroad Act on July 1, 1862. It endorsed the Central Pacific Railroad Company to build a line in California heading east.
The Pacific Railroad Act also chartered another rail line to lay tracks from the East. The Union Pacific Railroad Company was to build a line heading west from the Missouri River. The bill granted land and money for the project to both companies.
On January 8, 1863, California governor Leland Stanford broke ground for the line in Sacramento. The Central Pacific line began actual construction on October 26, 1863.

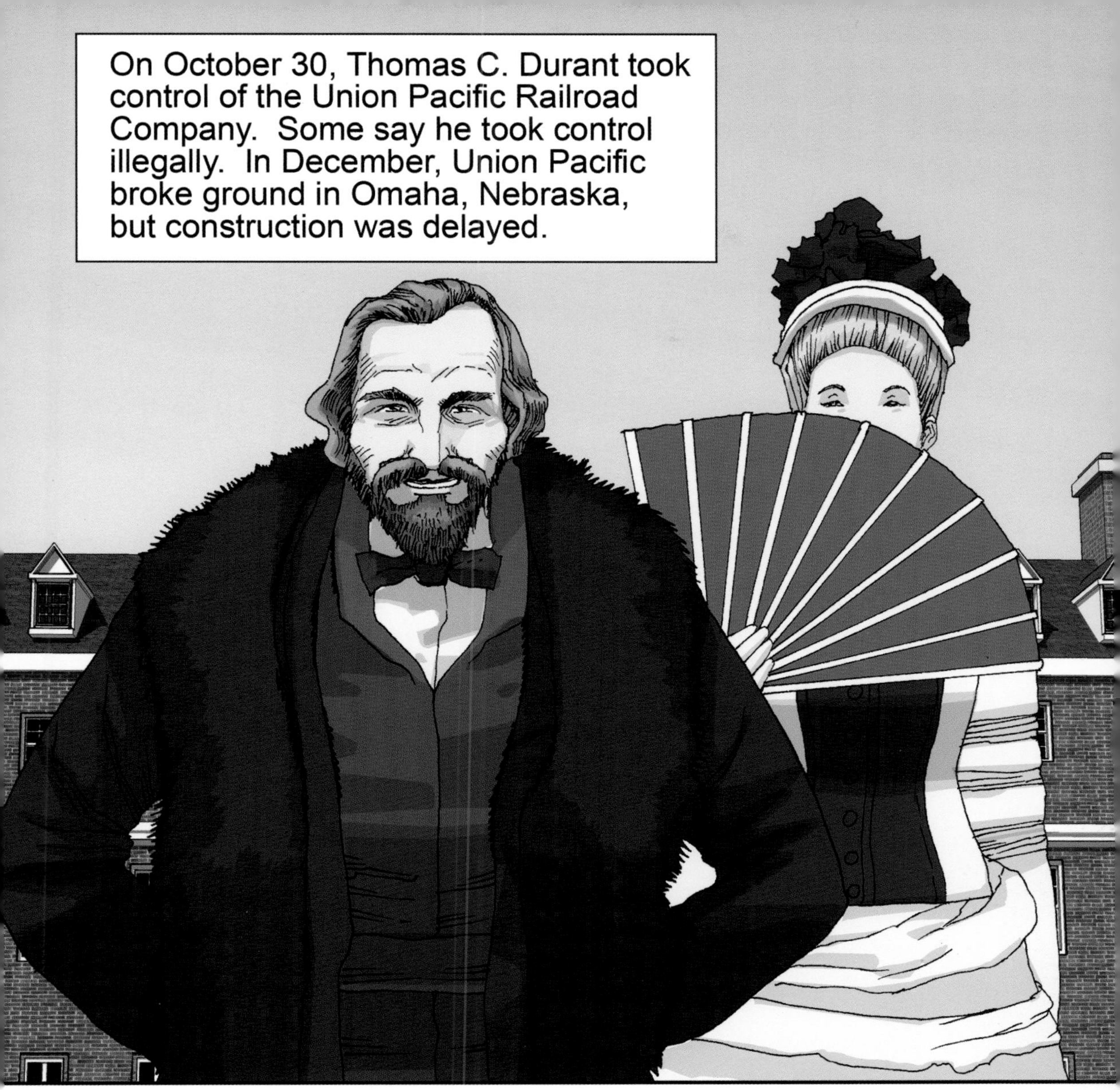
On October 30, Thomas C. Durant took control of the Union Pacific Railroad Company. Some say he took control illegally. In December, Union Pacific broke ground in Omaha, Nebraska, but construction was delayed.

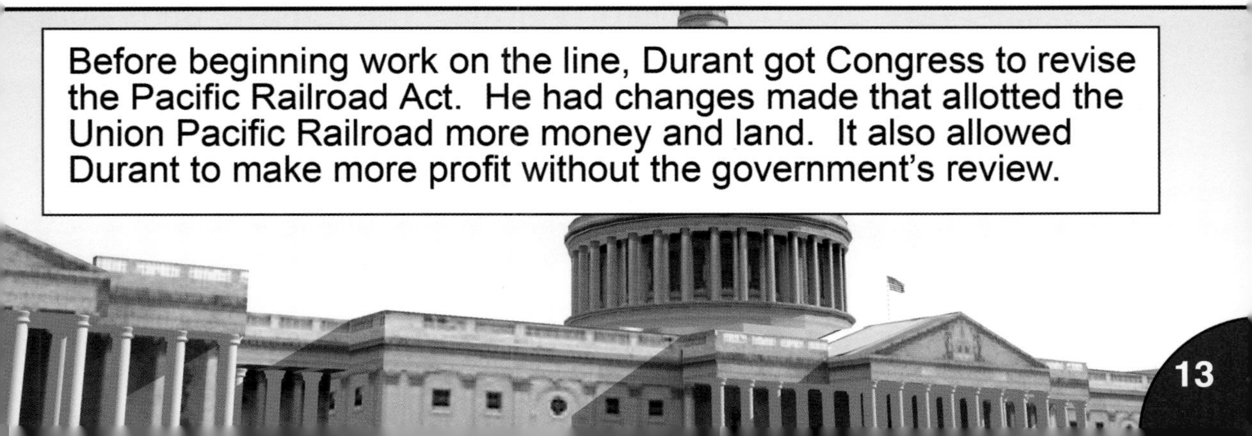
Before beginning work on the line, Durant got Congress to revise the Pacific Railroad Act. He had changes made that allotted the Union Pacific Railroad more money and land. It also allowed Durant to make more profit without the government's review.

Chapter 3 Construction Delays

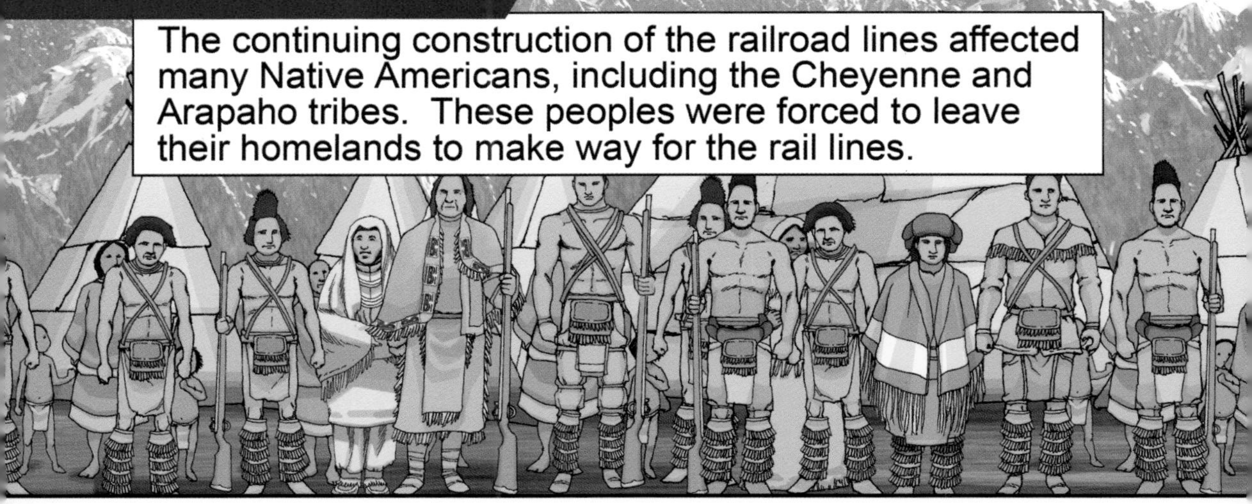
The continuing construction of the railroad lines affected many Native Americans, including the Cheyenne and Arapaho tribes. These peoples were forced to leave their homelands to make way for the rail lines.

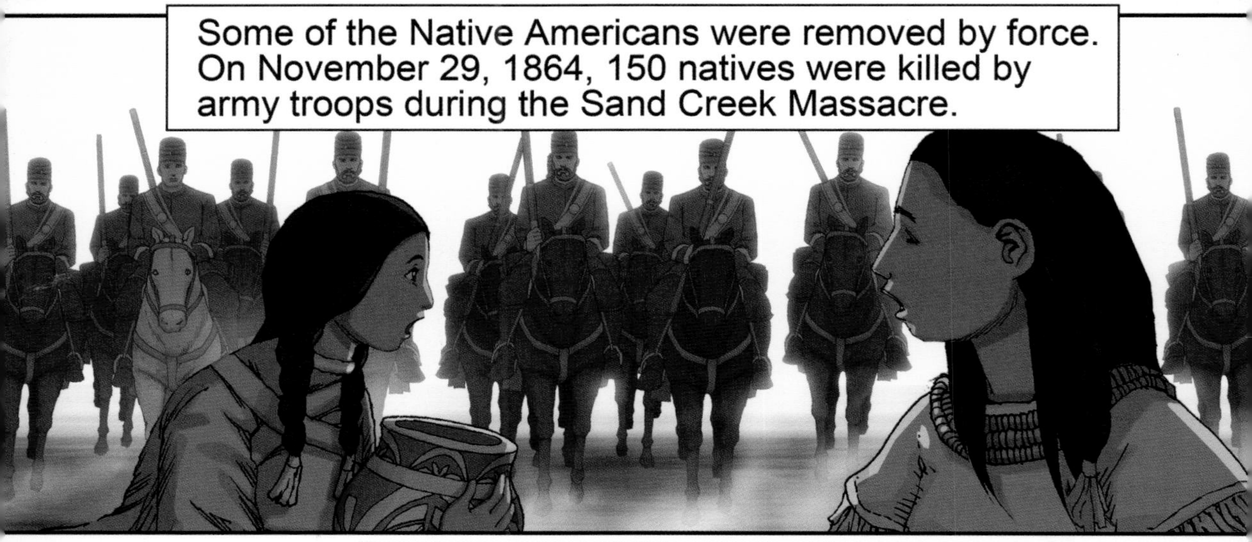
Some of the Native Americans were removed by force. On November 29, 1864, 150 natives were killed by army troops during the Sand Creek Massacre.

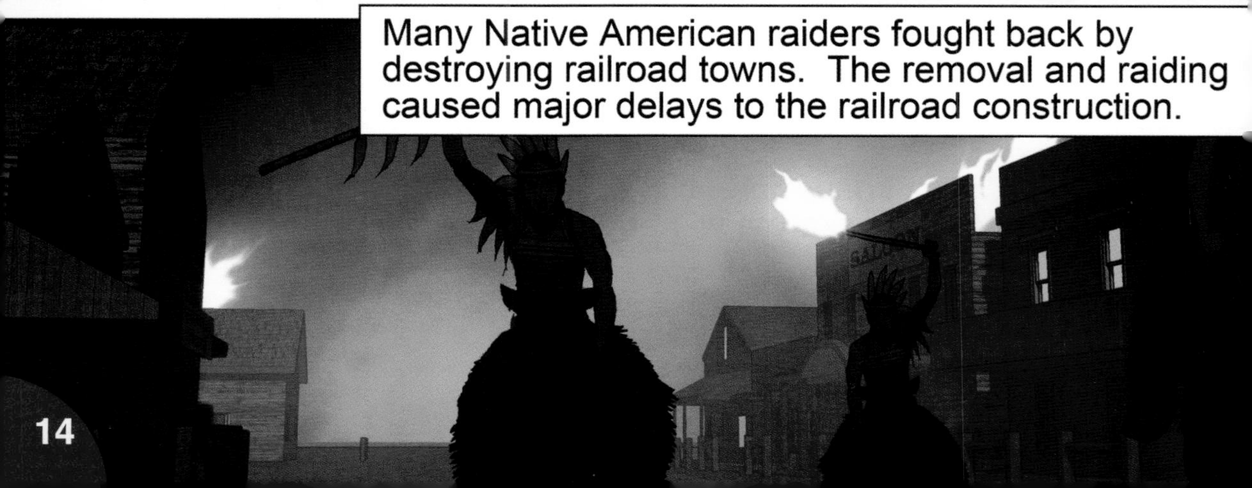
Many Native American raiders fought back by destroying railroad towns. The removal and raiding caused major delays to the railroad construction.

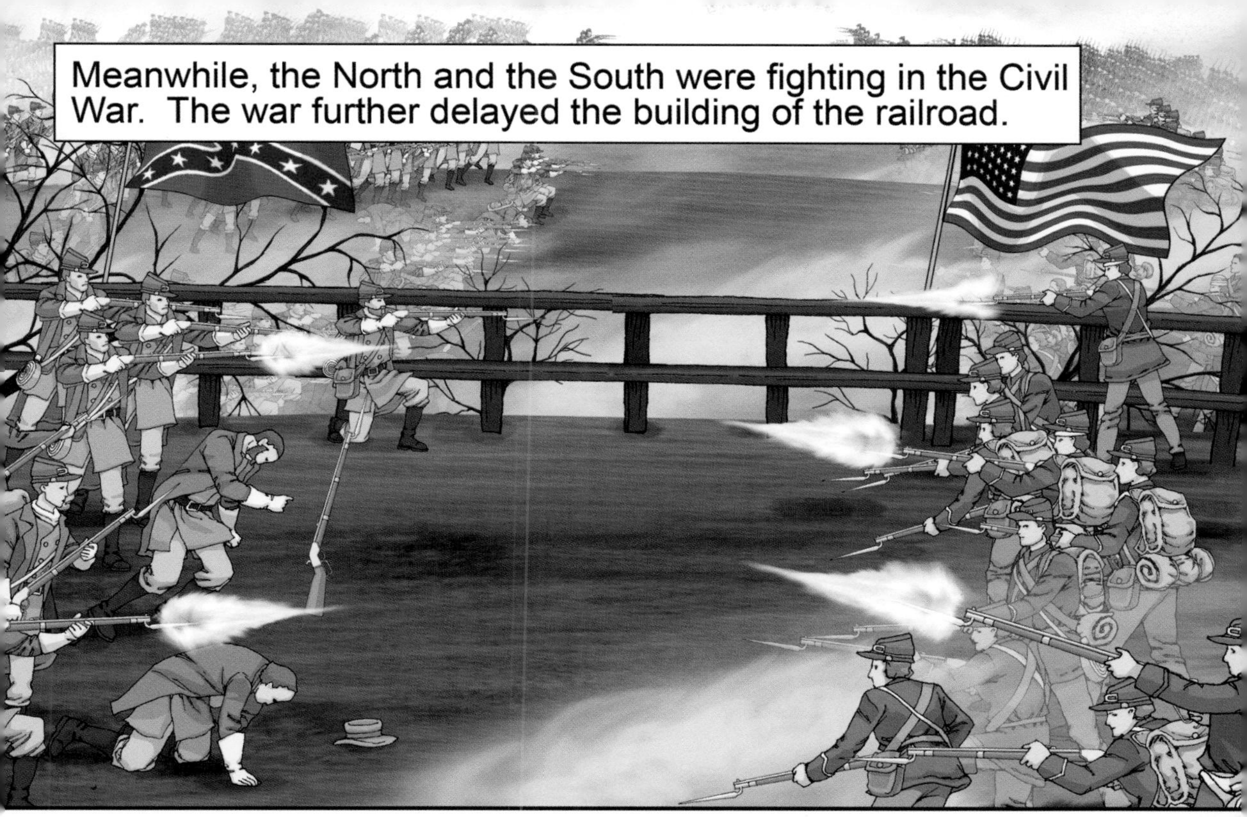
Meanwhile, the North and the South were fighting in the Civil War. The war further delayed the building of the railroad.

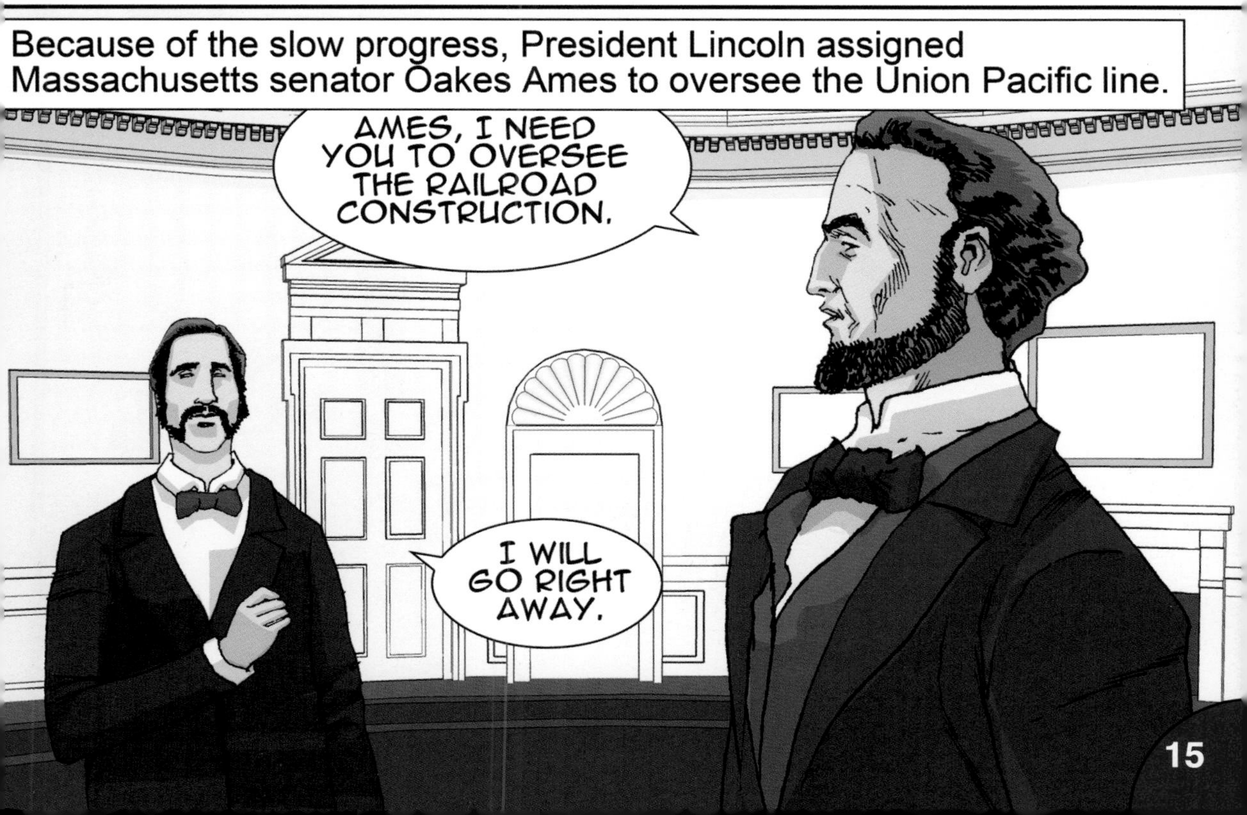
Because of the slow progress, President Lincoln assigned Massachusetts senator Oakes Ames to oversee the Union Pacific line.
AMES, I NEED YOU TO OVERSEE THE RAILROAD CONSTRUCTION.
I WILL GO RIGHT AWAY.

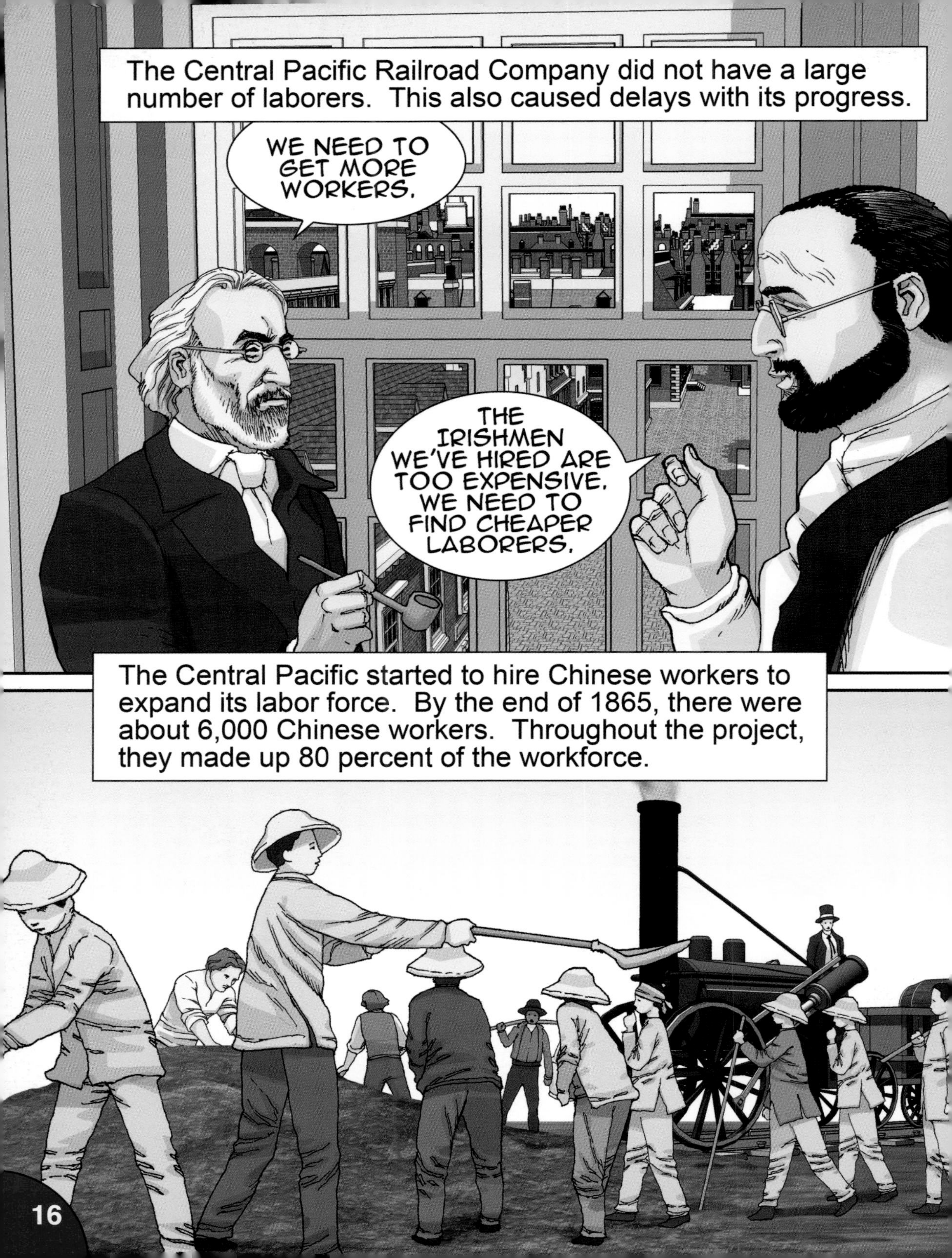
The Central Pacific Railroad Company did not have a large number of laborers. This also caused delays with its progress.
WE NEED TO GET MORE WORKERS.
THE IRISHMEN WE'VE HIRED ARE TOO EXPENSIVE. WE NEED TO FIND CHEAPER LABORERS.
The Central Pacific started to hire Chinese workers to expand its labor force. By the end of 1865, there were about 6,000 Chinese workers. Throughout the project, they made up 80 percent of the workforce.

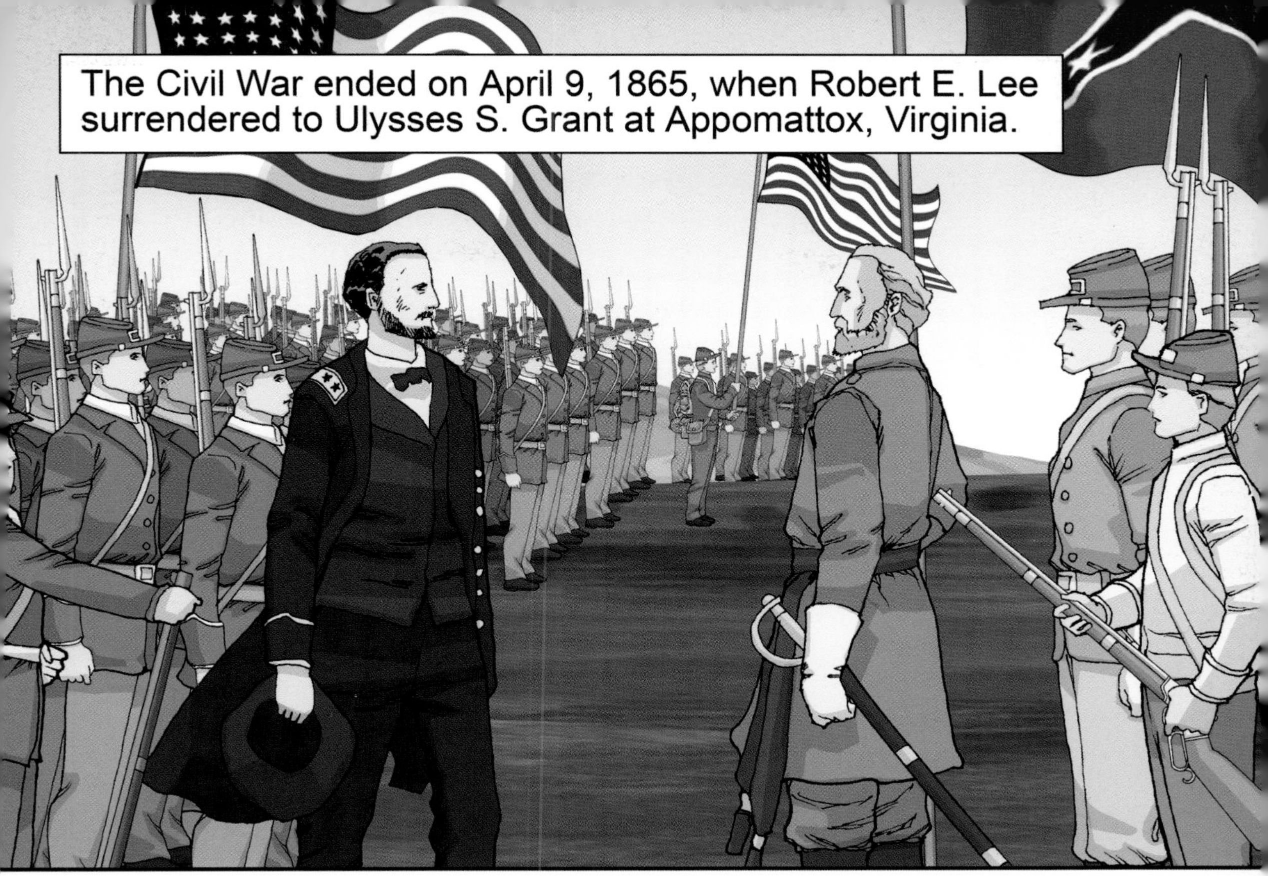
The Civil War ended on April 9, 1865, when Robert E. Lee surrendered to Ulysses S. Grant at Appomattox, Virginia.

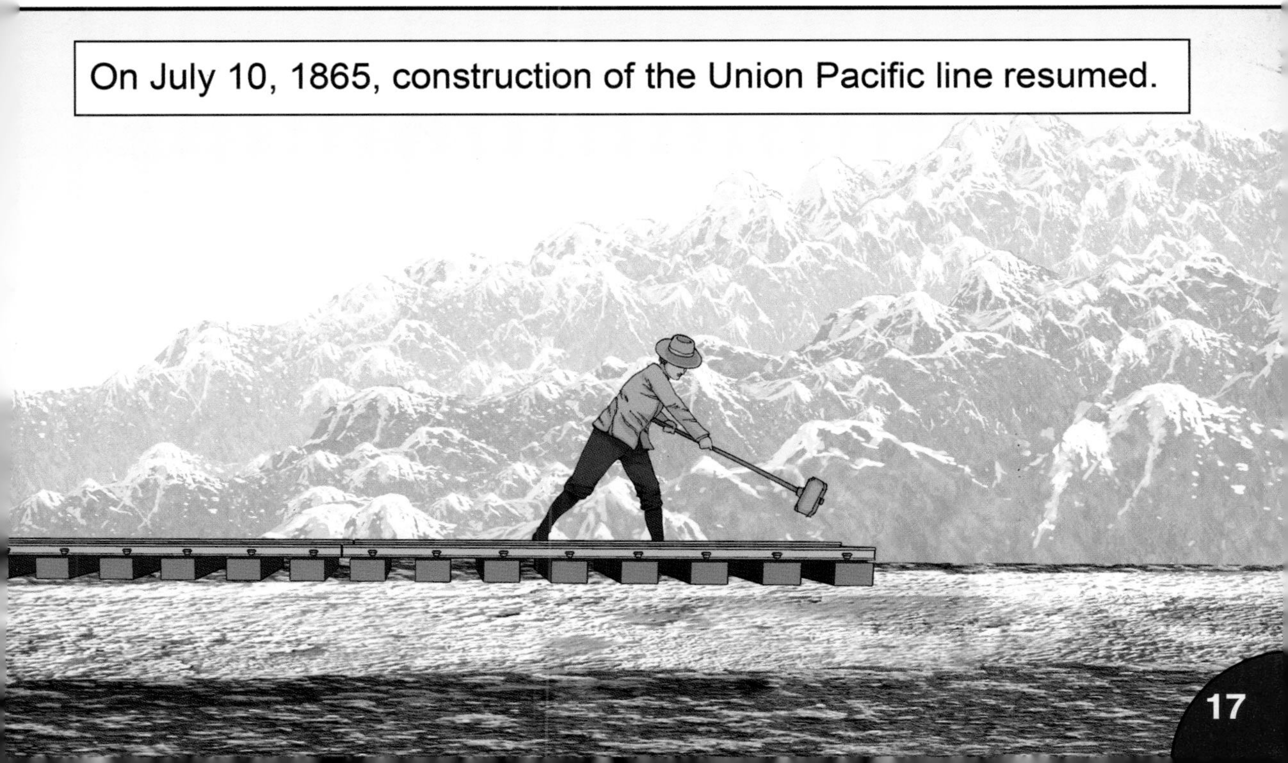
On July 10, 1865, construction of the Union Pacific line resumed.

Chapter 4 Union Pacific Advances

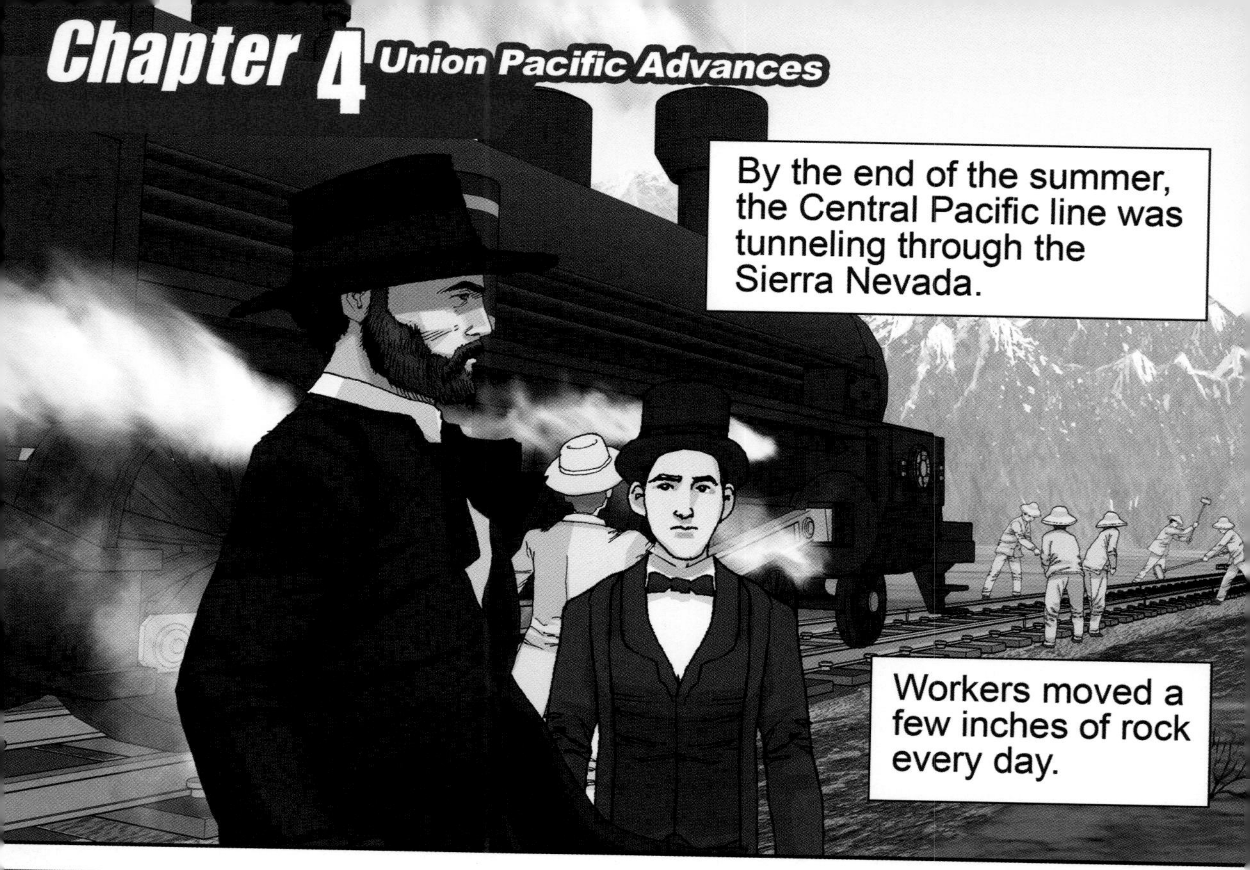
By the end of the summer, the Central Pacific line was tunneling through the Sierra Nevada.
Workers moved a few inches of rock every day.

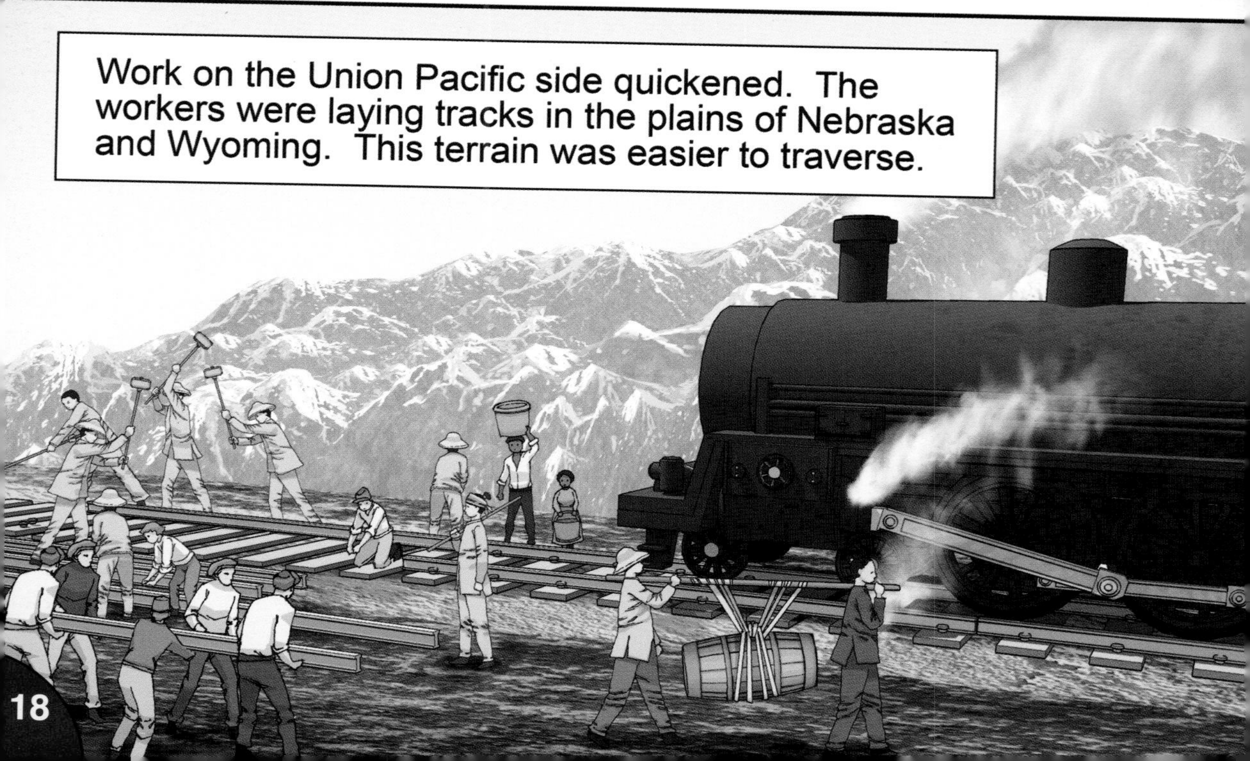
Work on the Union Pacific side quickened. The workers were laying tracks in the plains of Nebraska and Wyoming. This terrain was easier to traverse.

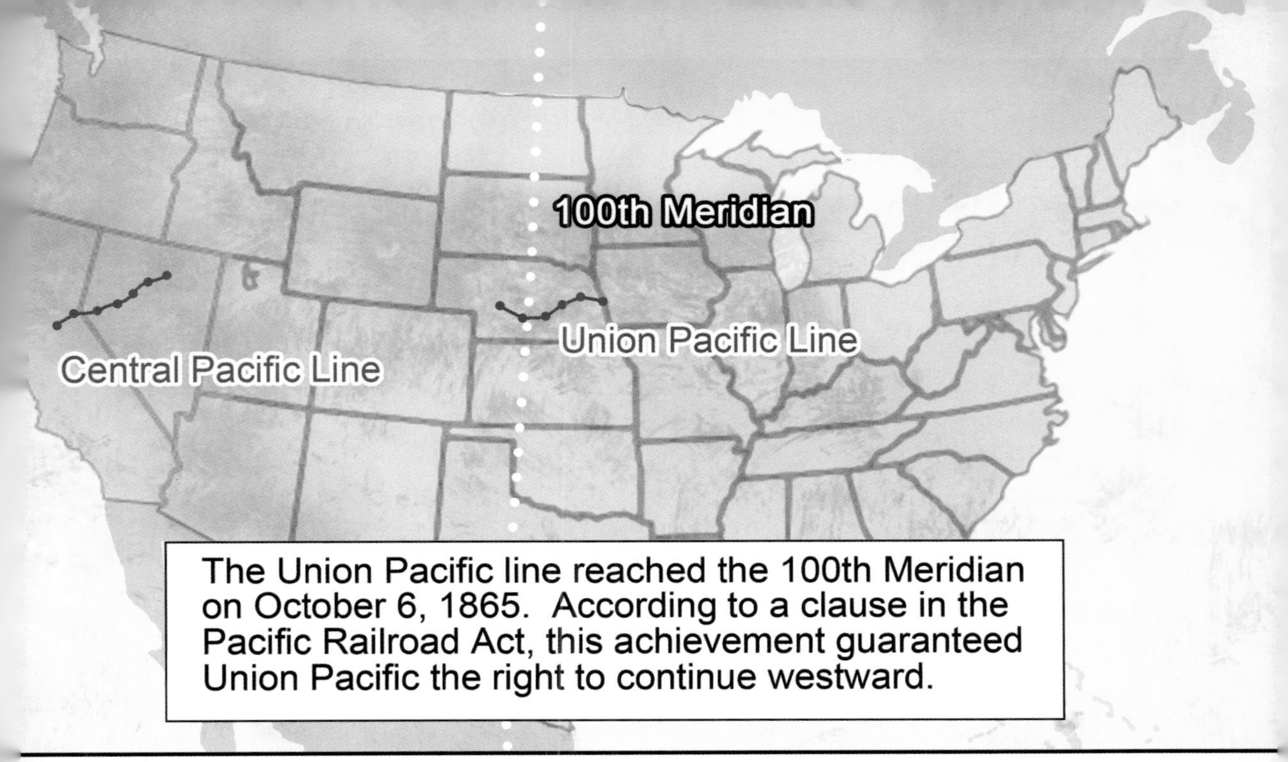
100th Meridian
Central Pacific Line
Union Pacific Line
The Union Pacific line reached the 100th Meridian on October 6, 1865. According to a clause in the Pacific Railroad Act, this achievement guaranteed Union Pacific the right to continue westward.

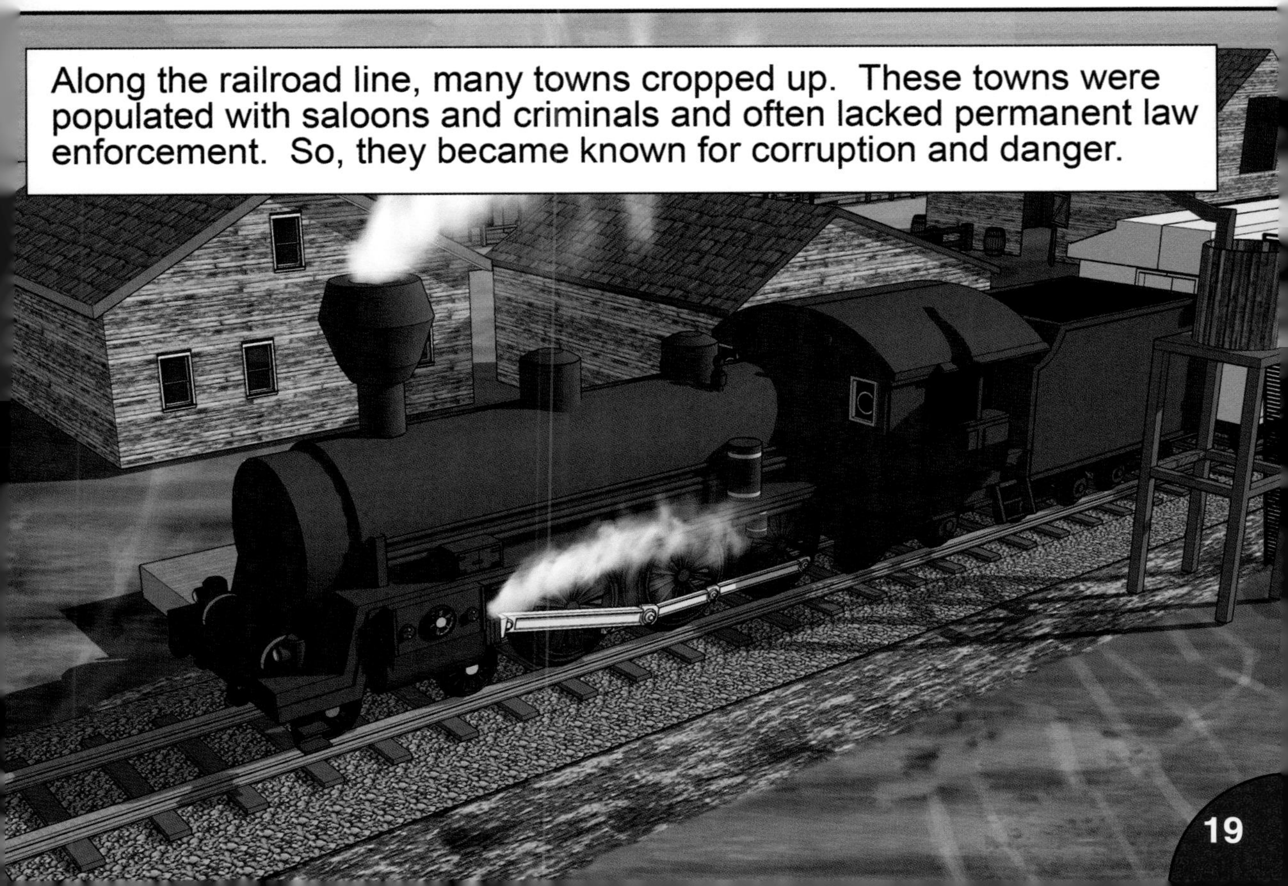
Along the railroad line, many towns cropped up. These towns were populated with saloons and criminals and often lacked permanent law enforcement. So, they became known for corruption and danger.

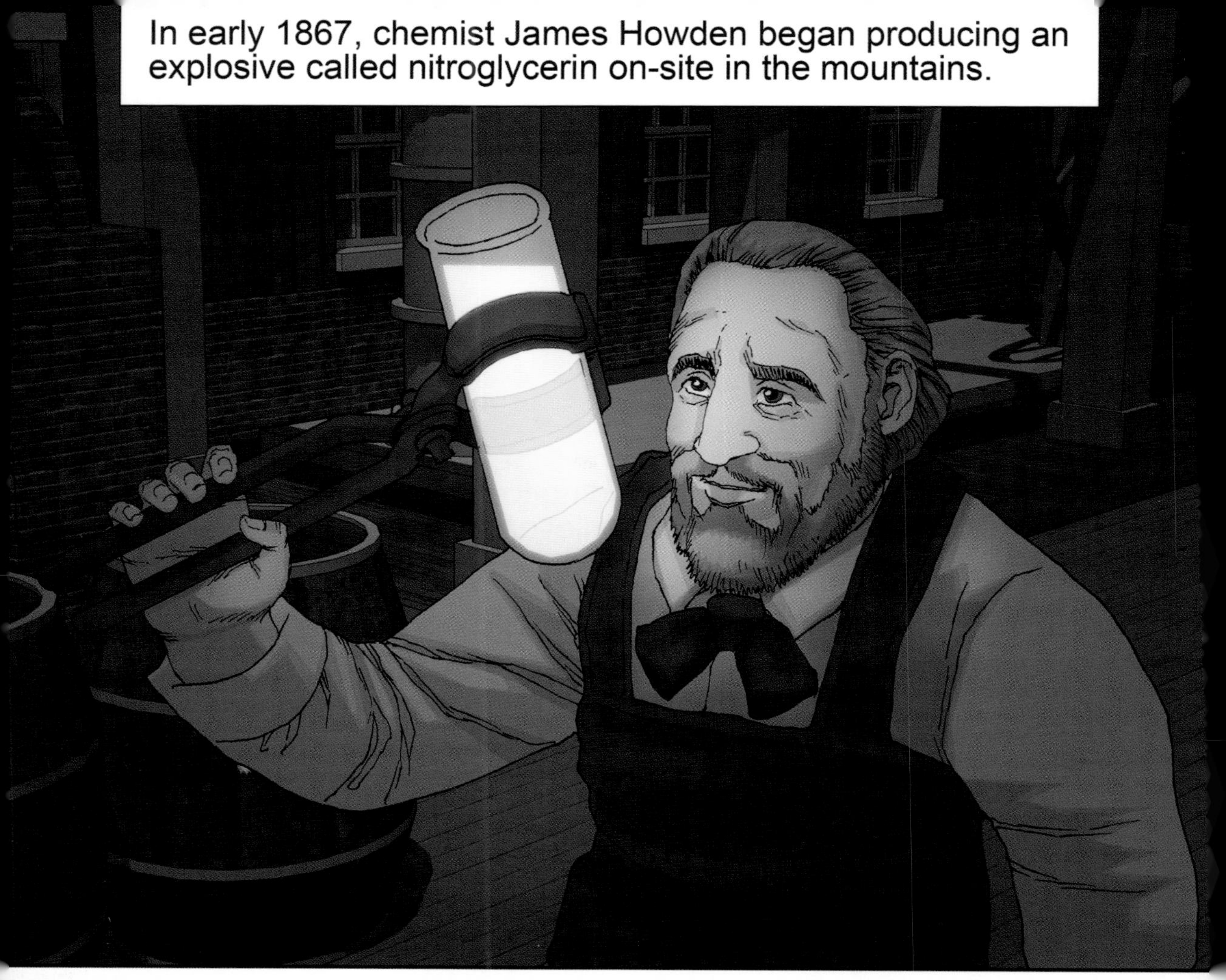
In early 1867, chemist James Howden began producing an explosive called nitroglycerin on-site in the mountains.

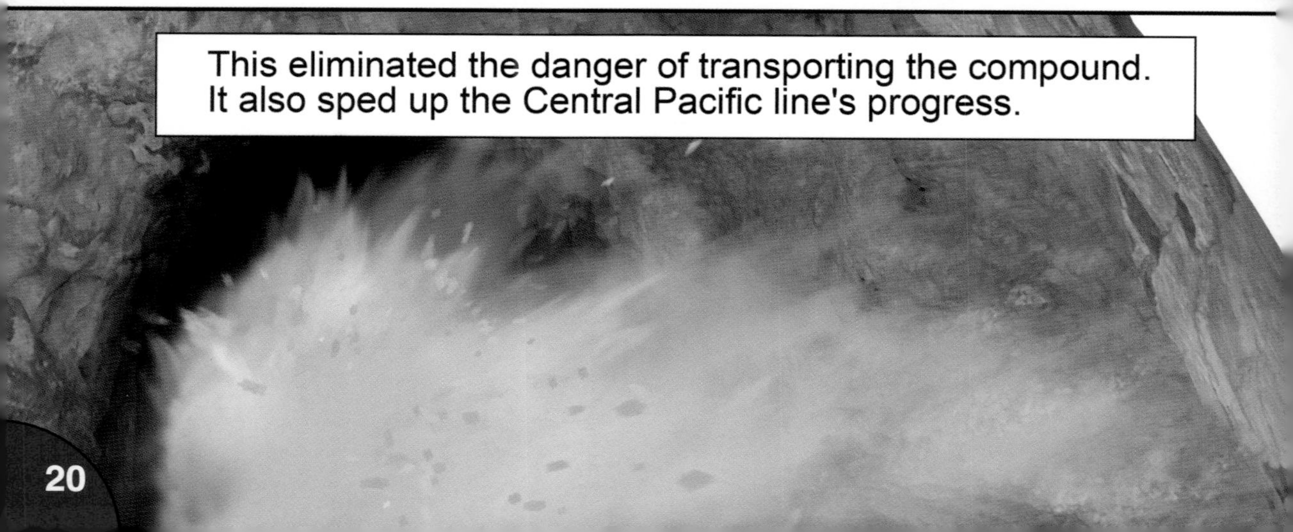
This eliminated the danger of transporting the compound. It also sped up the Central Pacific line's progress.

Chapter 5 Native Attacks

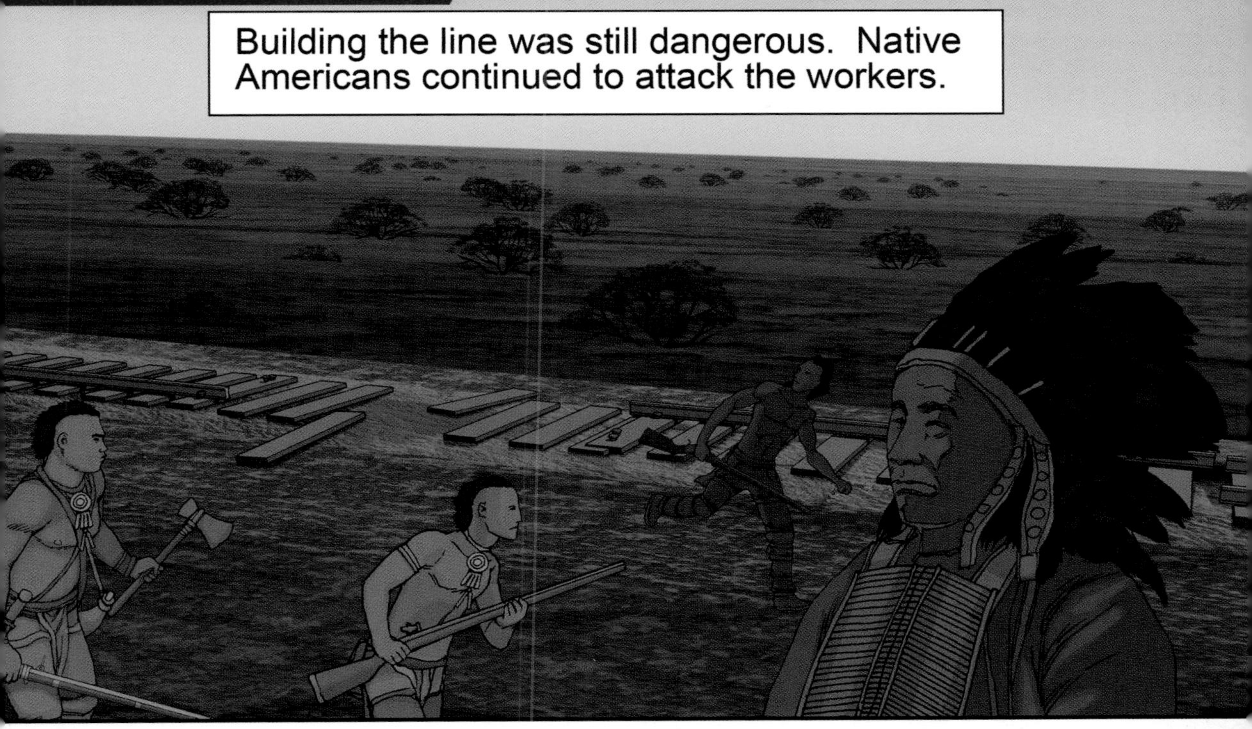
Building the line was still dangerous. Native Americans continued to attack the workers.

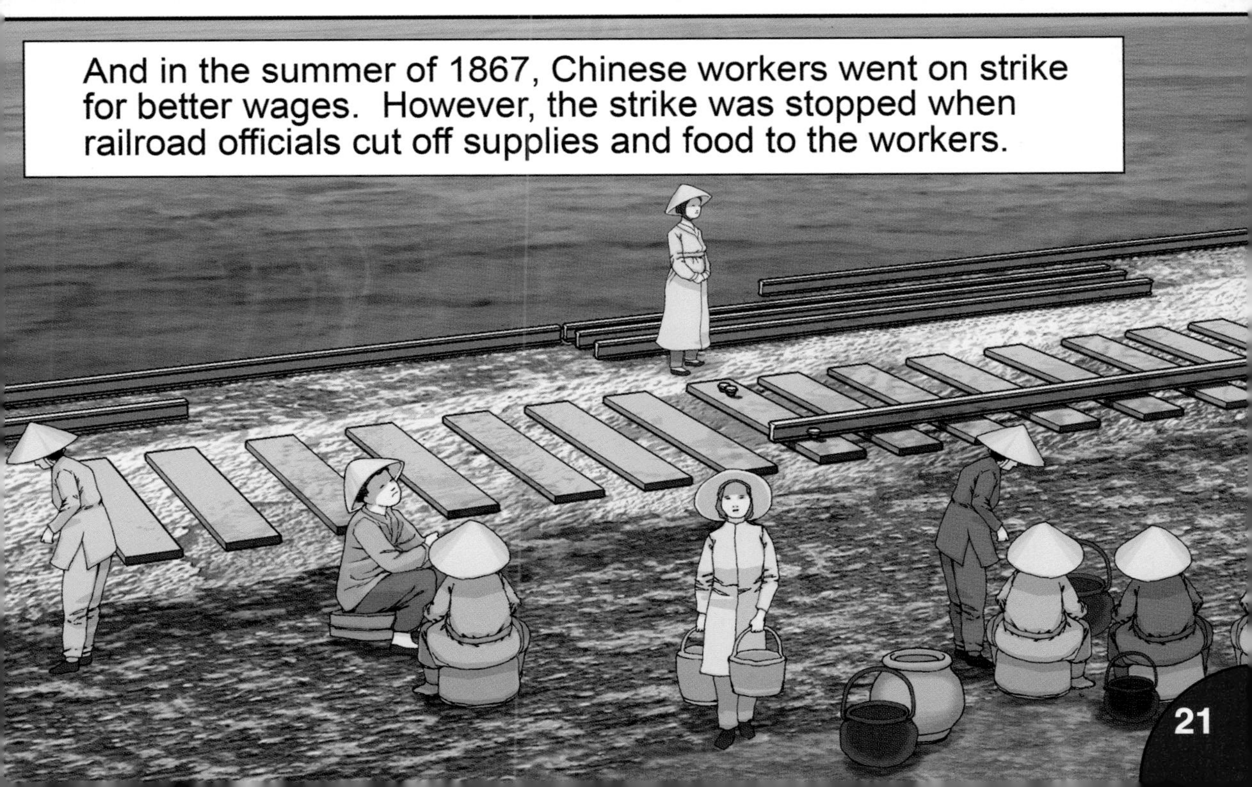
And in the summer of 1867, Chinese workers went on strike for better wages. However, the strike was stopped when railroad officials cut off supplies and food to the workers.

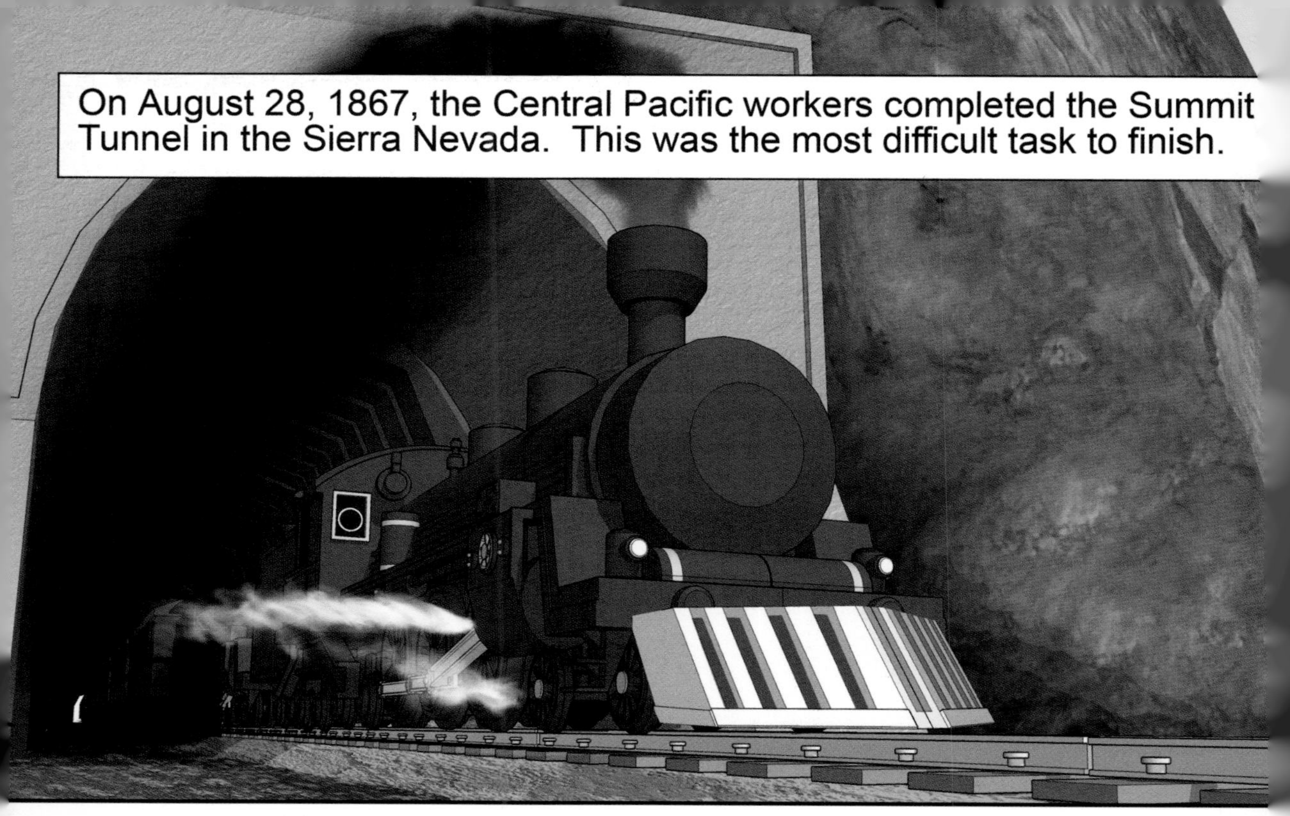
On August 28, 1867, the Central Pacific workers completed the Summit Tunnel in the Sierra Nevada. This was the most difficult task to finish.

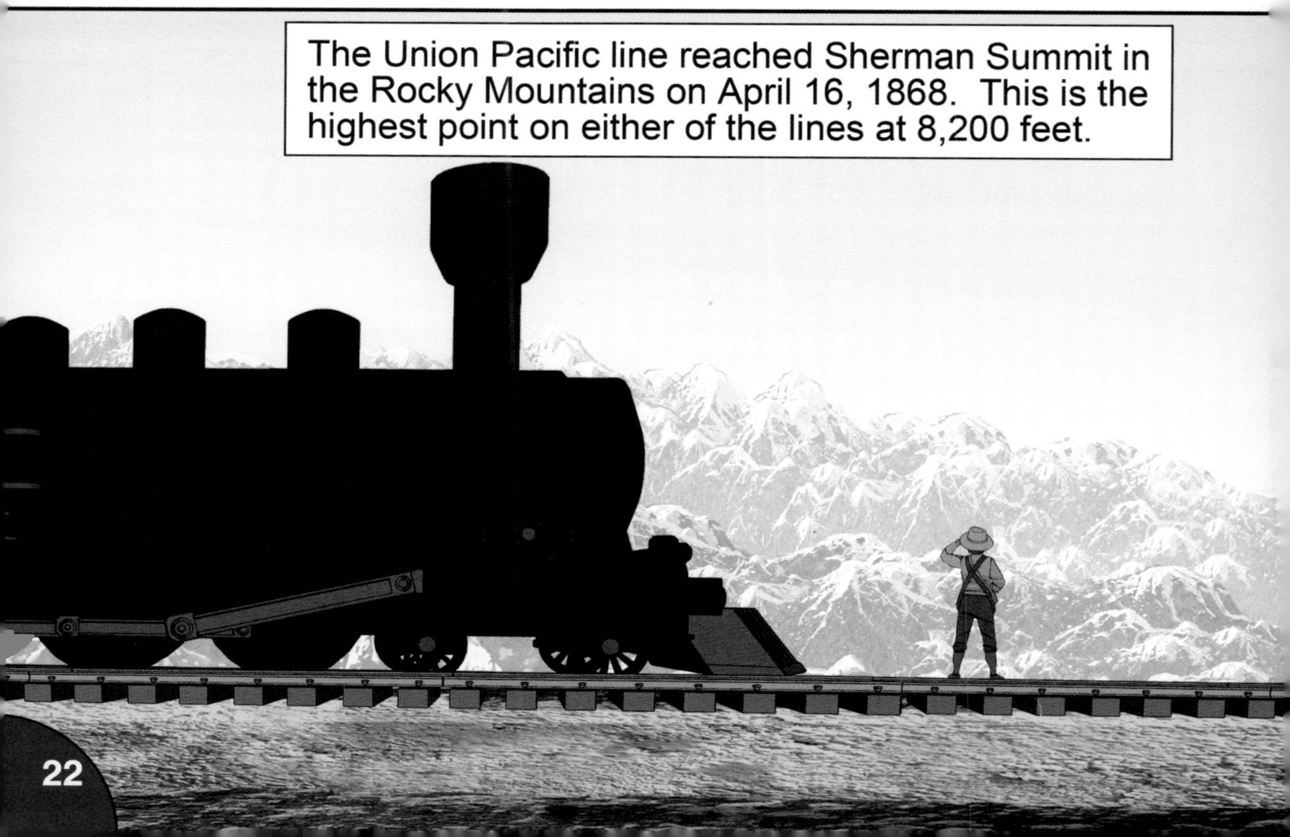
The Union Pacific line reached Sherman Summit in the Rocky Mountains on April 16, 1868. This is the highest point on either of the lines at 8,200 feet.

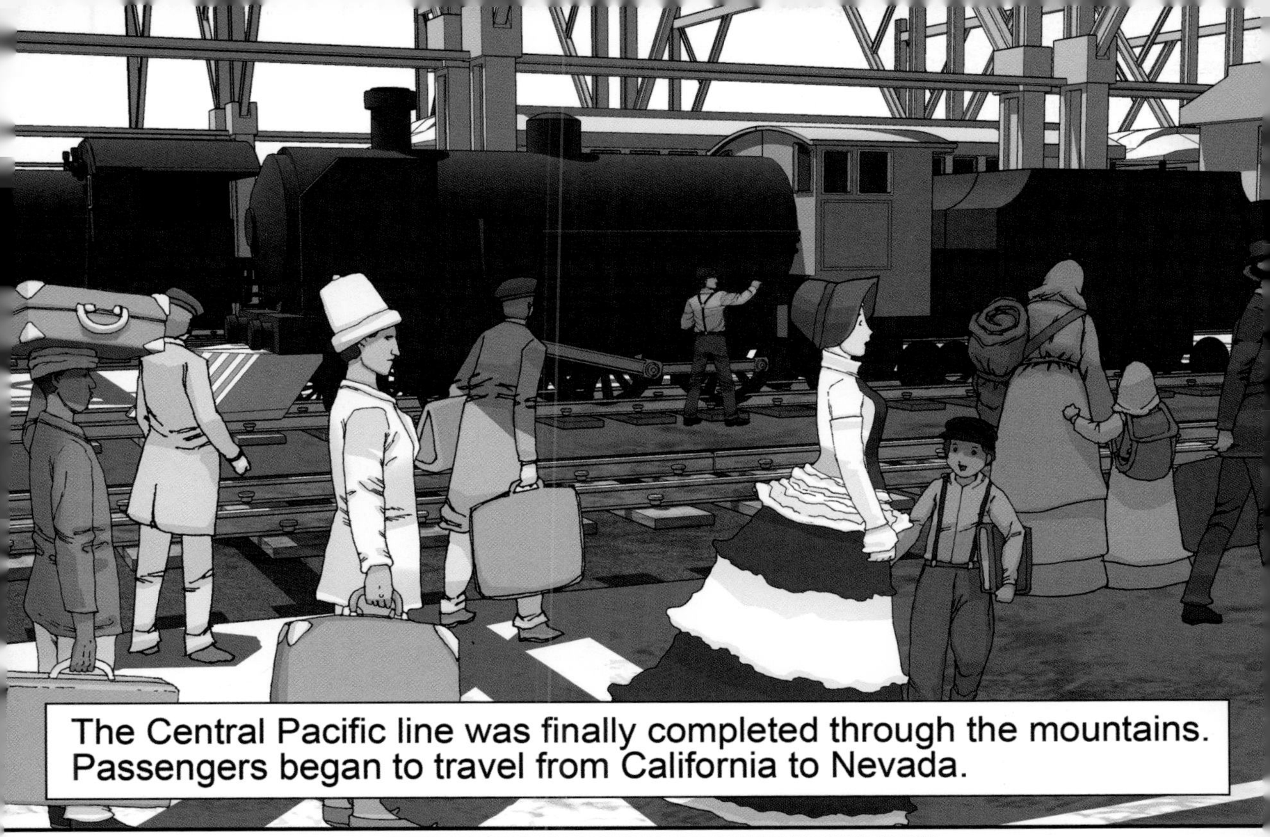
The Central Pacific line was finally completed through the mountains. Passengers began to travel from California to Nevada.

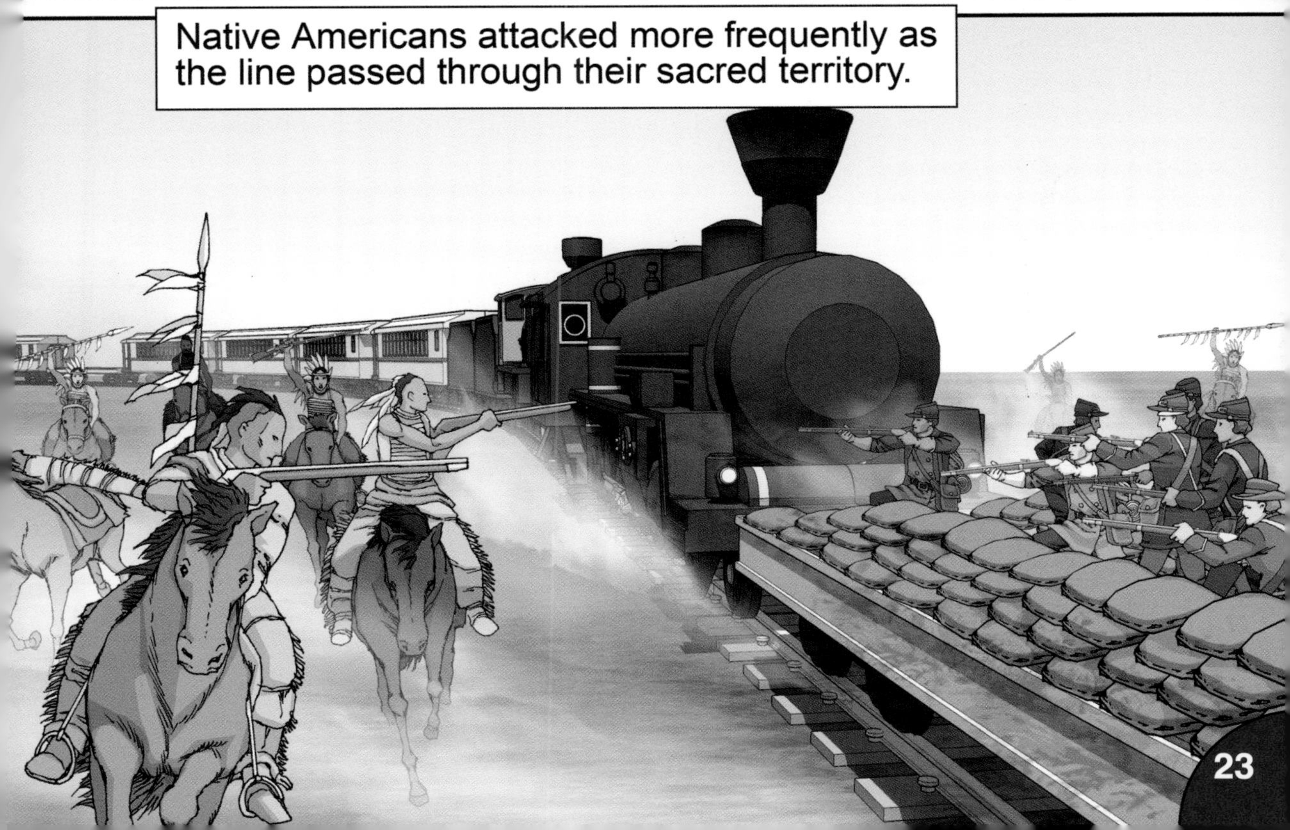
Native Americans attacked more frequently as the line passed through their sacred territory.

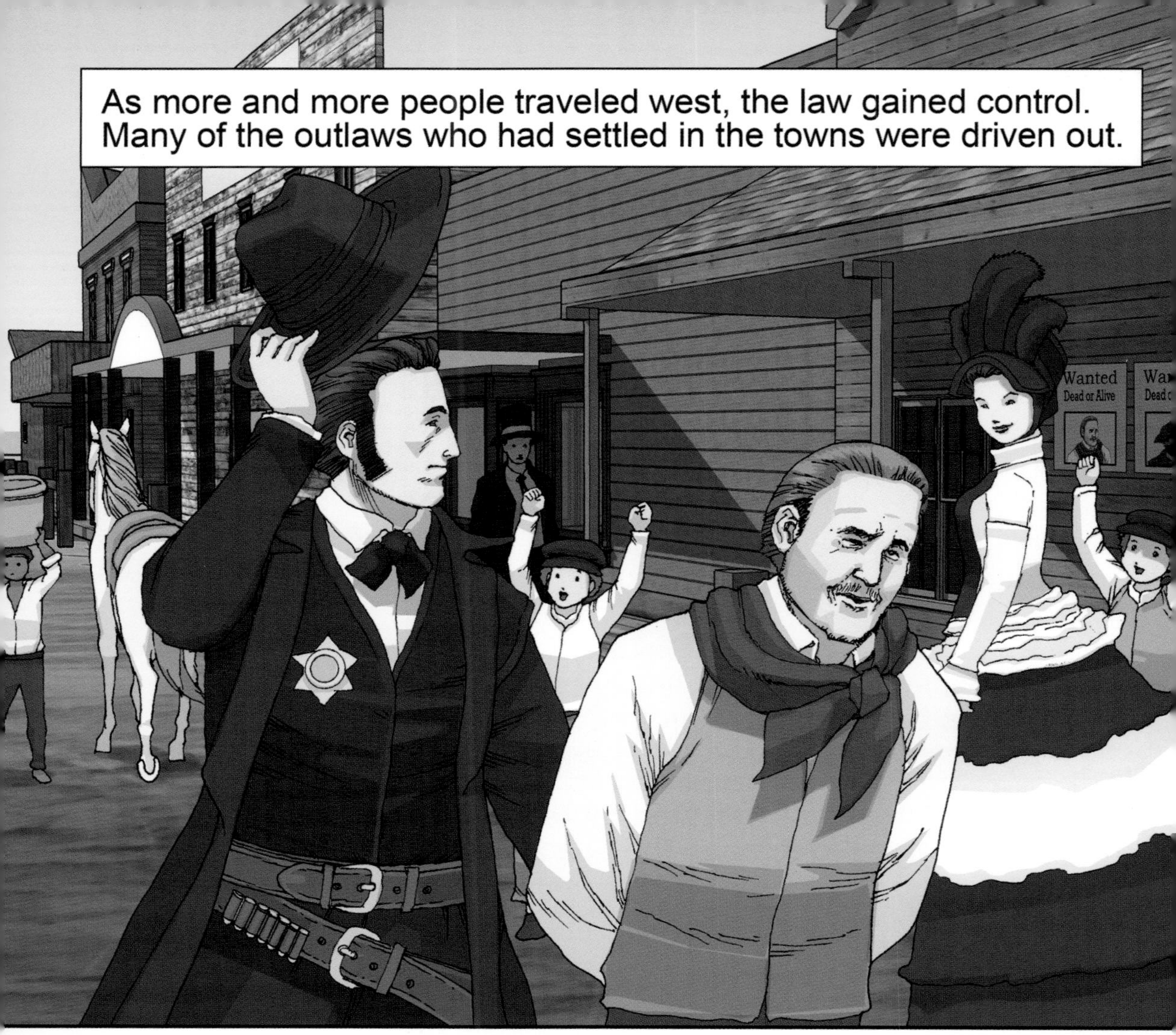
As more and more people traveled west, the law gained control. Many of the outlaws who had settled in the towns were driven out.
Wanted
Dead or Alive

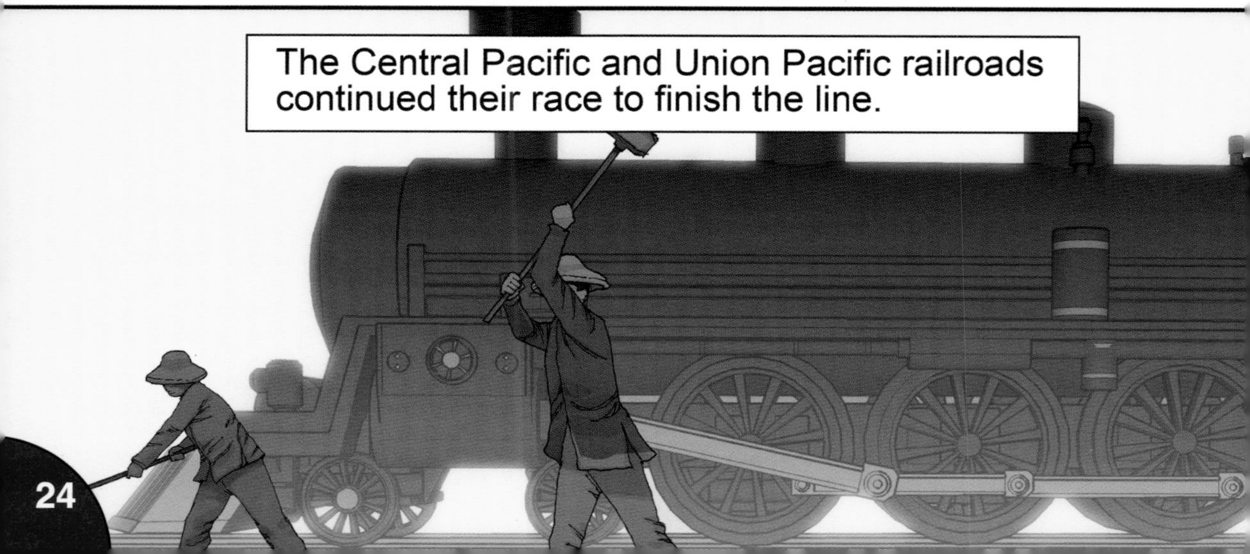
The Central Pacific and Union Pacific railroads continued their race to finish the line.

Chapter 6 Promontory Summit

As the lines approached each other, questions arose. The main question was where the two lines would meet.

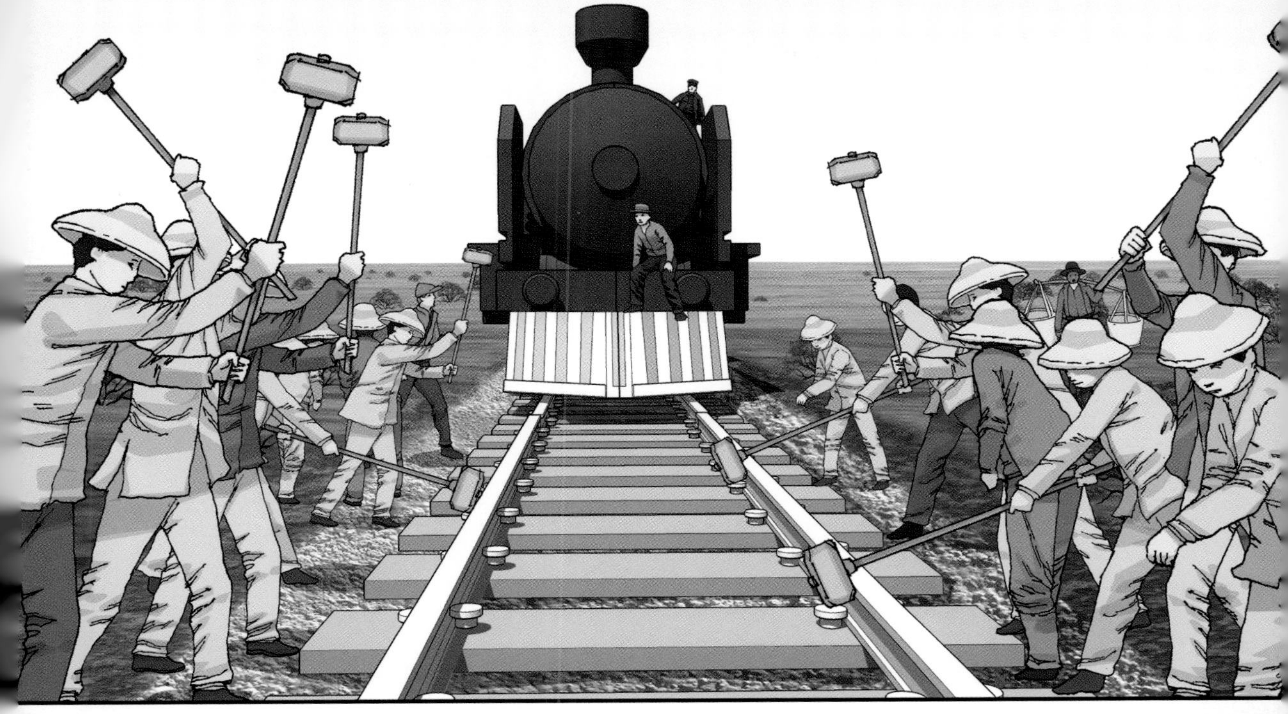

After two days of arguing over land, the railroad companies agreed to meet at Promontory Summit in Utah.

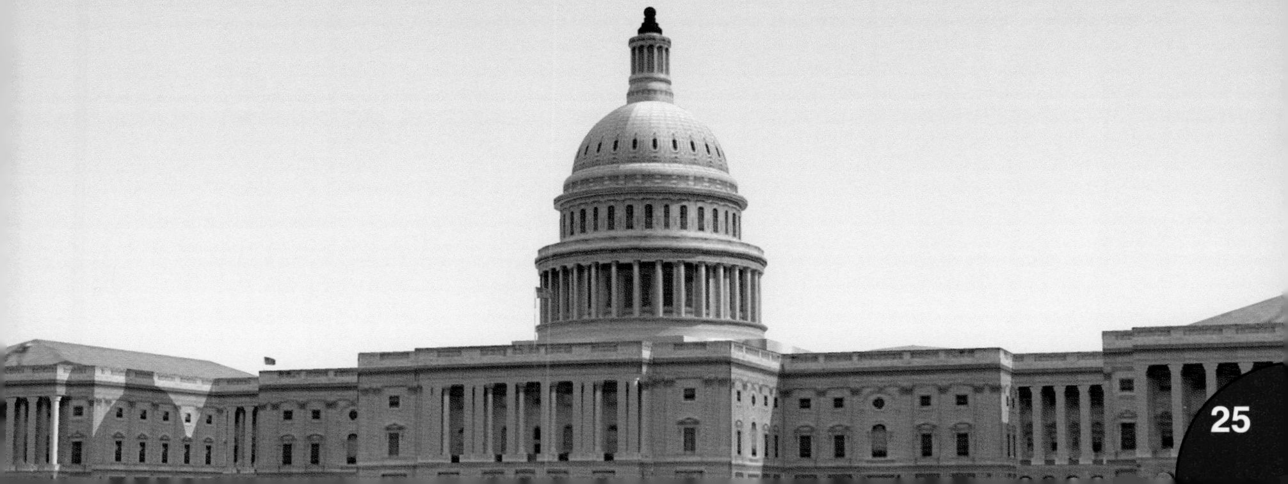

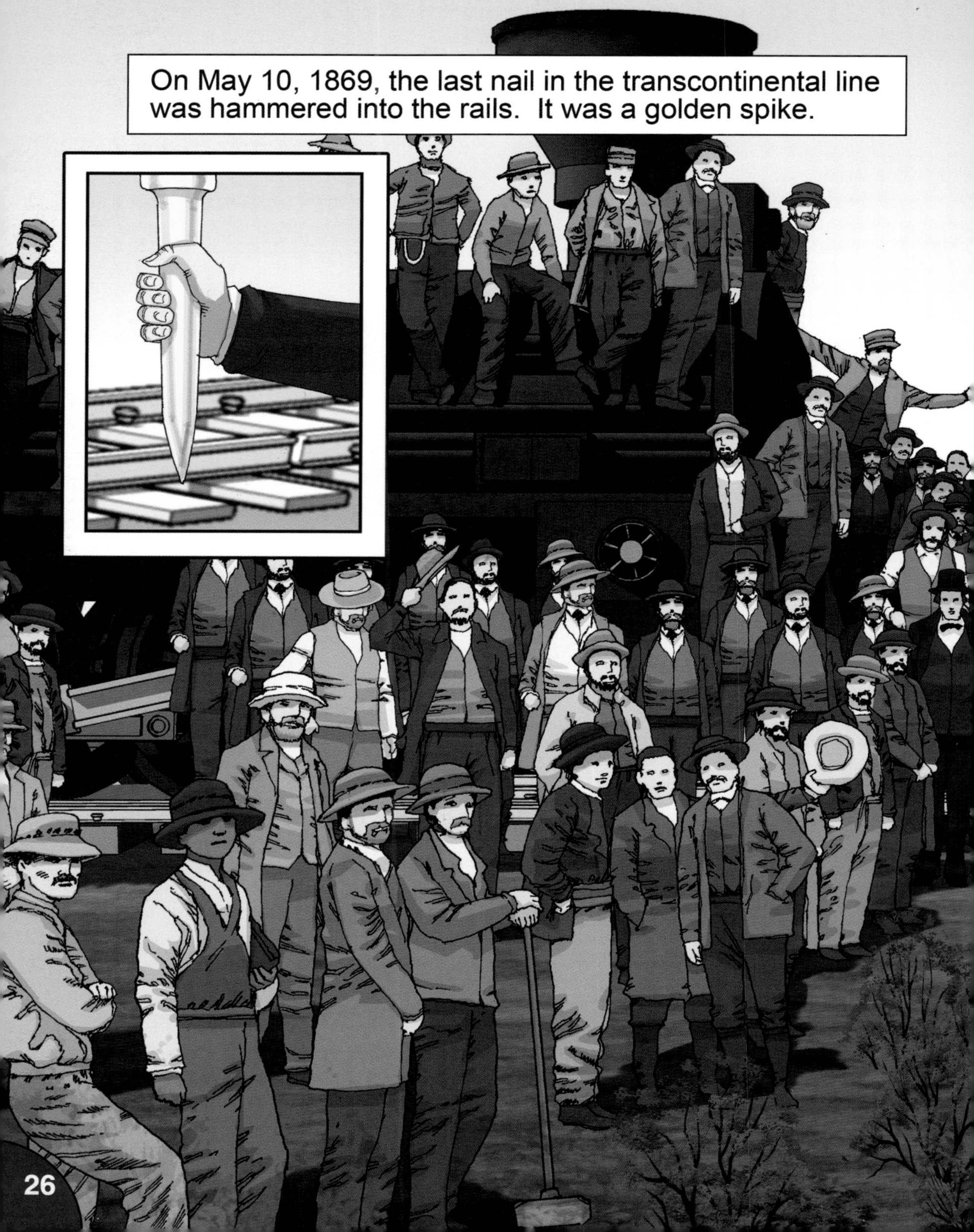
On May 10, 1869, the last nail in the transcontinental line was hammered into the rails. It was a golden spike.

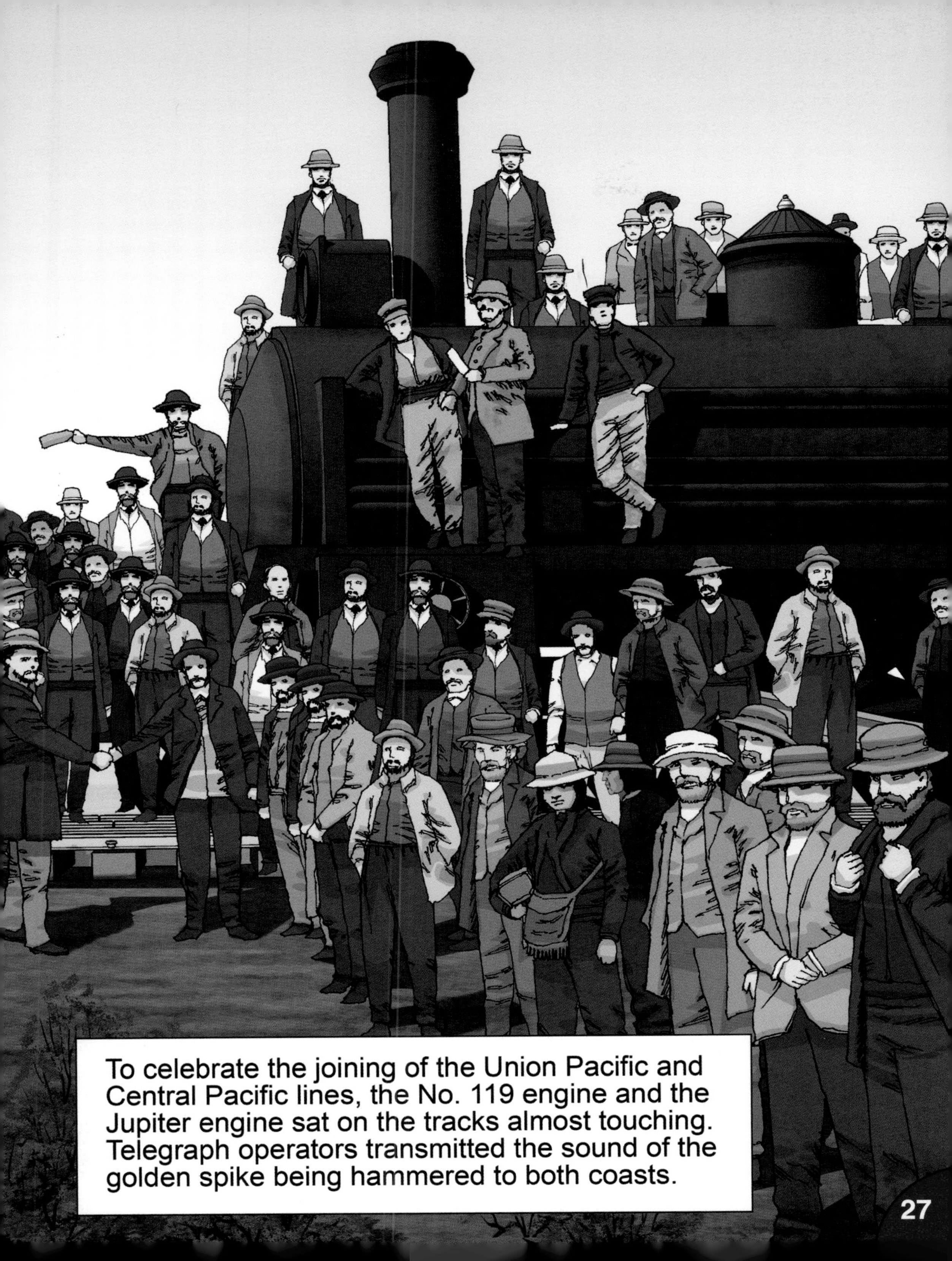
To celebrate the joining of the Union Pacific and Central Pacific lines, the No. 119 engine and the Jupiter engine sat on the tracks almost touching. Telegraph operators transmitted the sound of the golden spike being hammered to both coasts.

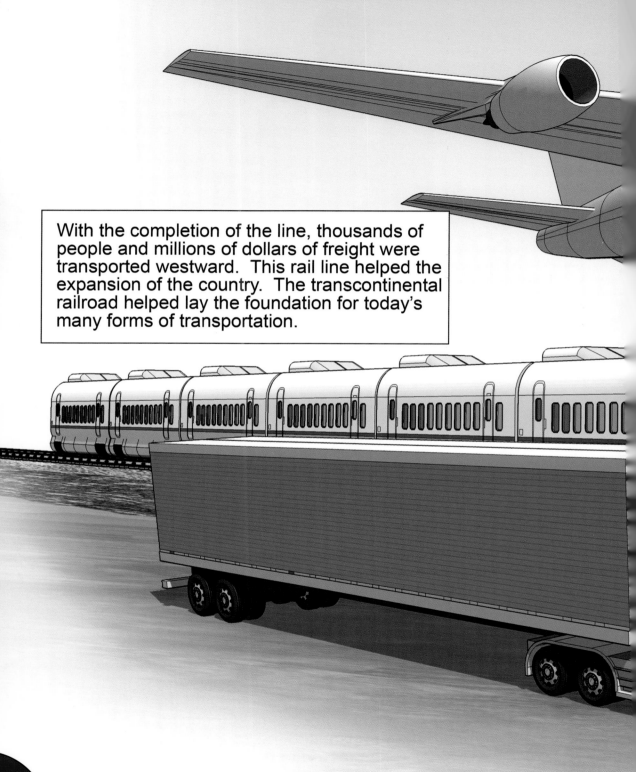

With the completion of the line, thousands of people and millions of dollars of freight were transported westward. This rail line helped the expansion of the country. The transcontinental railroad helped lay the foundation for today's many forms of transportation.

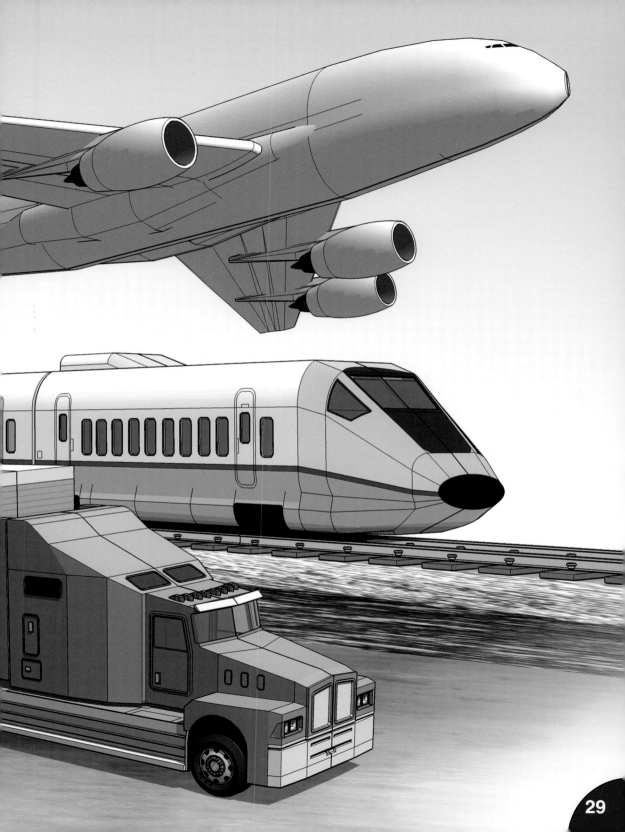

The Transcontinental Railroad

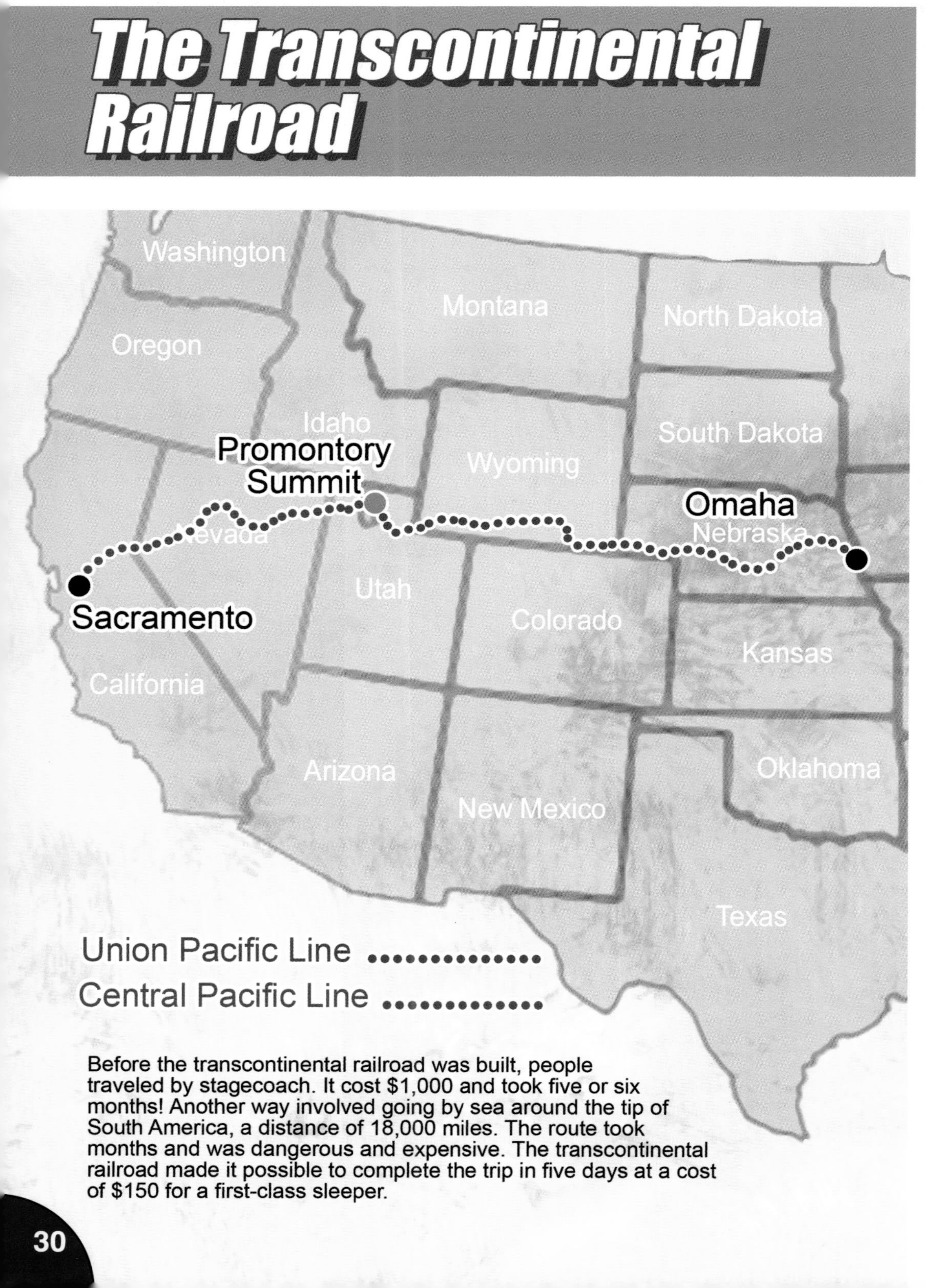
Washington
Montana
North Dakota
Oregon
Idaho
South Dakota
Promontory Summit
Wyoming
Omaha
Nevada
Nebraska
Sacramento
Utah
Colorado
Kansas
California
Arizona
Oklahoma
New Mexico
Texas
Union Pacific Line
Central Pacific Line

Before the transcontinental railroad was built, people traveled by stagecoach. It cost $1,000 and took five or six months! Another way involved going by sea around the tip of South America, a distance of 18,000 miles. The route took months and was dangerous and expensive. The transcontinental railroad made it possible to complete the trip in five days at a cost of $150 for a first-class sleeper.

Glossary

allot - to assign a share or portion of something.

charter - to hire, rent, or lease a guide or form of transportation.

civil war - a war between groups in the same country. The United States of America and the Confederate States of America fought a civil war from 1861 to 1865.

clause - a distinct article in a formal document.

corrupt - showing dishonest or improper behavior.

Industrial Revolution - the period in the 1800s when new machinery and technology changed the world economy.

meridian - a representation of a great circle that passes through the poles and is numbered for longitude on a map or globe.

surveyor - a person who measures a piece of land to determine its shape, area, and boundaries.

telegraph - a device that uses electricity to send coded messages over wires.

terrain - the physical features of an area of land. Mountains, rivers, and canyons can all be part of a terrain.

Web Sites

To learn more about the transcontinental railroad, visit ABDO Publishing Company on the World Wide Web at **www.abdopublishing.com.** Web sites about the transcontinental railroad are featured on our Book Links page. These links are routinely monitored and updated to provide the most current information available.

Index